Key Concepts in the Practice of
Sufism

Emerald Hills of the Heart

1

Revised Edition

M. Fethullah Gülen

ᴛʜᴇ Fountain

New Jersey-2004

Published by The Light, Inc.

42 Park Ave.

Rutherford, NJ 07070 USA

www.thelightinc.com

contact@thelightinc.com

Translated by Ali Unal

Library of Congress Cataloging-in-Publication Data is available

ISBN 1-932099-23-9

Printed and bound

by Caglayan A.S, Izmir-Turkey

September 2004

989904CA/1321

Printed and bound
by Seçil Ofset İstanbul-Turkey
100. Yıl Matbaacılar Sitesi 4. Cadde No: 77 Bağcılar Tel.: (0212) 629 06 15 (pbx)

Table of Contents

Author's Biography

Known for his simple and austere lifestyle, M. Fethullah Gülen, affectionately called Hodjaefendi, is a renowned, important scholar, a prolific writer and poet. This man for all seasons was born in Erzurum, eastern Turkey, in 1941. Upon graduation from divinity school, he obtained his license to preach and in his sermons he underlined the importance of understanding and tolerance, in addition to moral and spiritual values. His social reform efforts, begun during the 1960s, have made him one of Turkey's most well-known and respected public figures. His tireless dedication to solving social problems and satisfying spiritual needs have gained him millions of followers throughout the world.

Though simple in outward appearance, he is original in thought and action. He embraces all humanity, and is deeply averse to unbelief, injustice, and deviation. His belief and feelings are profound, and his ideas and approach to problems are both wise and rational. A living model of love, ardor, and feeling, he is extraordinarily balanced in his thoughts, acts, and treatment of matters.

He is acknowledged, either tacitly or explicitly, by Turkish intellectuals and scholars as one of the most serious and important thinkers and writers, and among the wisest activists of modern Turkey or even of the Muslim world. But such accolades of his leadership of a new Islamic intellectual, social, and spiritual revival—a revival with a potential to embrace great areas of the world—do not deter him from striving to be no more than a humble servant of God and a friend to all. Desire for fame is the same as show and ostentation, a "poisonous honey" that extinguishes the heart's spiritual liveliness; is one of the golden rules he follows.

Gülen has spent his adult life voicing the cries and laments, as well as the belief and aspirations, of Muslims in particular, and of humanity in general. He is able to bear his own sorrows, but those of others crush him. He feels each blow delivered to humanity as delivered first to his own heart. He feels himself so deeply and inwardly connected to creation that he once said: "Whenever I see a leaf fall from its branch in autumn, I feel as much pain as if my arm had been amputated."

M. Fethullah Gülen and His Mission

After completing his education, Gülen taught in Edirne and was active in religious and social services. After doing his military service and teaching for some time in Edirne, he was transferred to Izmir, which proved to be a turning-point in his life. It was during this time that his total dedication to religious life and his interest in the general human condition became apparent. While in Izmir, he began to travel from city to city to speak on subjects ranging from Darwinism to social justice in Islam, and to visit places where people gathered to convey his message.

Applaud the good for their goodness; appreciate those
who have believing hearts; be kind to the believers.
Approach unbelievers so gently that
their envy and hatred melt away;
like a Messiah, revive people with your breath.

Gülen dreamed of a generation that would combine intellectual "enlightenment" with pure spirituality, wisdom, and continuous activism. Being extraordinarily knowledgeable in religious and social sciences and familiar with the principles of "material" sciences, he instructed his students in most of these areas. The first students who attended his courses in Izmir became the vanguard of a revived generation willing to serve his ideals. The small group that had begun to form around his opinions by the end of 1960s has increased rapidly and steadily ever since.

The generation captivated by his tears and sincerity, altruism and love, continues to serve without thought of material reward.

They preach, teach, and establish private educational institutions all over the world; they publish books, magazines and newspapers; they participate in television and radio broadcasts, and fund scholarships for poor students. Completely apolitical, they have founded and are operating hundreds of schools and universities from Denmark to Australia, the United States and Russia, Japan and South America. They also operate a television channel that broadcasts from Turkey to a wide area including the United States, Central Asia, and Australia.

> *Only those who overflow with love*
> *will build the happy and enlightened world of the future.*
> *Their lips smiling with love, their hearts brimming with love,*
> *their eyes radiating love and the most tender human feelings*
> *- such are the heroes of love who continuously receive messages of love*
> *from the rising and setting of the sun*
> *and from the flickering light of the stars.*

Further remarks

Gülen is well-known for his ardent endeavor to strengthen bonds among people. He maintains that there are more bonds bringing people together than those separating them. Based on this belief, he works without rest for a sincere, sound dialogue and tolerance. He was one of the founders of the Foundation of Journalists and Writers, a group that promotes dialogue and tolerance among all social strata and which has received a warm welcome from almost all walks of life. He regularly visits and receives leading Turkish and international figures: the Vatican Ambassador to Turkey, the Patriarch of the Turkish Orthodox Community, the Patriarch of the Turkish Armenian Community, the Chief Rabbi of the Turkish Jewish Community, as well as leading journalists, columnists, television and movie stars, and thinkers of varying views.

M. Fethullah Gülen asserts that if you wish to keep the masses under control, simply starve them of knowledge. They can escape such tyranny only through education. He believes that the road to social justice is paved with adequate, universal education, for only this will give people sufficient understanding and tolerance to respect the rights of others. To this end, he has encouraged community leaders, the elite of society, industrialists, and business leaders to support quality education for the needy.

Be so tolerant that your bosom becomes wide like the ocean.
Become inspired with faith and love of human beings.
Let there be no troubled souls to whom
you do not offer a hand and about whom
you remain unconcerned.

His efforts have begun to bear fruit, as graduates from the private schools in Turkey and Central Asia established by some Turkish private donations and run as trusts, have taken top honors in university placement tests and consistently finish at the top in International Knowledge Olympics. They have produced several world champions, especially in mathematics, physics, chemistry, and biology.

A man is truly human only if he learns
and teaches, and inspires others. It is difficult to regard
as truly human someone who is ignorant and has
no desire to learn. It is also questionable
whether a learned person who does not renew
and reform himself so as to set an example
for others is truly human.

M. Fethullah Gülen maintains, "If a nation expects to be ignorant and free in a state of civilization, it expects what never was and never will be." In education, he has inspired the use of mass media, notably television, to inform those without a formal education of pressing social matters.

"As a political and governing system, democracy is the only alternative left in the world," he maintains. In spite of its many shortcomings, he says that no one has yet designed a better governing system. So, we must make it work. People shall always demand freedom of choice in their affairs, especially in their expression of spiritual and religious values.

There is a mutually supportive and perfective relation
between an individual's actions and his inner life.
We may call it a "virtuous circle." Attitudes like
determination, perseverance, and resolve illuminate
his inner conscience; the brightness of his
inner conscience strengthens his will-power
and resolve stimulates him to higher horizons.

"Do not despair in the face of adversity, and do not yield to anarchists," he emphasizes, lest we give up hope. To him, hopelessness is a quicksand that buries human progress and kills the will to succeed, a noose that chokes and drowns people.

With his acute perception, Gülen perceives that the world's spiritual climate is undergoing a positive change. He envisions a twenty-first century in which we will see the sprouting of a spiritual dynamic that will revive the now-dormant moral values. He envisions an age of tolerance and understanding that will lead to the cooperation of civilizations and their ultimate fusion into one body. The human spirit shall triumph in the form of intercivilizational dialogue and the sharing of values.

Gülen successfully bridges the past with his image of the future. His deep desire to find a solution for contemporary social problems has resulted in pearl-like sentences set one after another in his writings and speeches; priceless pearls on a string. In his inimitable style and choice of vocabulary, he offers a way out of the "material quicksand" in which humanity finds itself today.

A soul without love cannot be elevated to the horizon
of human perfection. Even if he were to live hundreds of years,
he could make no advance on the path of perfection.
Those who are deprived of love, entangled in
the nets of selfishness, are unable to love anybody else and
die unaware of the love deeply implanted
in the very being of existence.

"Today's people are in search of their Creator and the reason for their creation," Gülen contends. He gives practical, convincing answers to such questions as: Why was I born? What is the purpose of my life? What is the meaning of death, and what does it demand from me? In his speeches and writings, one encounters statements like: "Humanity has reached a crossroads: one leads to despair, the other to salvation. May God give us the wisdom to make the right choice." His works represent a search for the truth.

He does not believe that there are any material shortages in the world, and sees no justification for starvation. Inequitably distributed wealth should be channeled through private charities to the needy. He has spearheaded the establishment of many charitable organizations to do just that.

At a time when humanity is in acute need of leaders, we find a true innovator and leader in M. Fethullah Gülen. A unique social reformer, he has synthesized the positive sciences with divinity, reconciling all "apparent" differences between the two. In his writings and speeches, he brings the ideologies and philosophies of East and West closer together.

> Compassion is the beginning of being; without it
> everything is chaos. Everything has come into
> existence through compassion, and by compassion
> it continues to exist in harmony. The earth was put
> in order by messages coming from the other
> side of the heavens. Everything from the macrocosm
> to the microcosm has achieved an extraordinary
> harmony thanks to compassion.

"As for getting others to accept your ways," M. Fethullah Gülen tells us, "the days of getting things done by brute force are over. In today's enlightened world, the only way to get others to accept your ideas is by persuasion and convincing arguments. Those who resort to brute force to reach their goal are intellectually bankrupt souls." In their daily lives, people must maintain the delicate balance between material and spiritual values if they are to enjoy serenity and true happiness. Unbridled greed must be guarded against.

A true leader who leads by example, he lives as he preaches and presents an ideal living model to emulate. A student of *hadith, tafsir, fiqh,* Sufism, and philosophy, he occupies his rightful place among his contemporaries in Islamic sciences.

At the present time, he continues his efforts for a better future for the whole humanity. He teaches Islamic sciences to a large group of graduate divinity students under his private tutelage, and has a large following in Turkey, where he is believed to be one of the six most influential and respected personalities. His recently published biography already has reached its fiftieth edition.

Love is the most essential element in every being,
and it is a most radiant light and a great power
which can resist and overcome every force.
Love elevates every soul which absorbs it,
and prepares it for the journey to eternity.
Souls which have been able to make contact with
eternity through love, exert themselves
to implant in all other souls what they
receive from eternity. They dedicate their
lives to this sacred duty, for the sake of which
they endure every kind of hardship to the end,
and just as they pronounce "love" with
their last breath, they also breathe love
while being raised on the Day of Judgment.

His Works

Throughout his life, M. Fethullah Gülen has tasted almost nothing of worldly pleasure. He has spent his bachelor life studying, teaching, travelling, writing, and speaking. He always feels the sufferings of people coming from the spiritual wasteland of the twentieth century.

In addition to his books, Gülen contributes to several journals and magazines. He writes the editorial page for *Sizinti*, *Yeni Umit*, *Yagmur*, and *The Fountain* magazines. His sermons and discourses have been recorded on thousands of tapes and video cassettes. In addition, many books have been compiled from his articles, sermons, and the answers to questions he has been asked over the years. Some of his books are as follows:

· *Asrin Getirdigi Tereddutler* (4 volumes; vol. I has appeared in English translation as *Questions and Answers About Faith*)

- *Kalbin Zumrut Tepeleri* (translated as *Emerald Hills of the Heart: Key Concepts in the Practice of Sufism*)

- *Cag ve Nesil* ("This Era and the Young Generation")

- *Olcu Veya Yoldaki Isiklar*, (4 volumes; vol. 1 has appeared in English translation as *Pearls of Wisdom*)

- *Zamanin Altin Dilimi* ("The Golden Part of Time")

- *Renkler Kusaginda Hakikat Tomurcuklari* (2 volumes; vol. 1 has appeared in English translation as *Truth through Colours*)

- *Kirik Mizrap* ("Broken Plectrum"), a collection of verse

- *Fatiha Uzerine Mulahazalar* ("The Interpretation of Sura al-Fatiha")

- *Sonsuz Nur* (2 volumes, translated as *Prophet Muhammad, Aspects of His Life*)

- *Yitirilmis Cennet'e Dogru* (translated as *Towards the Lost Paradise*)

- *Inancin Golgesinde* (translated as *Understanding and Belief: Essentials of the Islamic Faith*)

Some of Hodjaefendi's books, among them *Kirik Mizrap*, *Inancin Golgesinde* and *Asrin Getirdigi Tereddutler*, have been translated into many other languages such as Arabic, German, Russian, Albanian, Bulgarian, and Indonesian.

Editor's Preface

The various stages of the Sufi Path are introduced and described in this book. Those readers who are not familiar with Islam or Sufism should be aware of the following points.

First, men and women begin to follow the Sufi path when they sense there is something more to Islam than what appears on the surface, or in a desire to get nearer to God. They act on this desire by following a stricter way of self-purification in order to penetrate the "inner" dimension and meaning of Islamic rituals, to reach a deeper understanding of the meaning and purposes of the Divine acts, and to thereby acquire knowledge and love of God. When this point is reached, God begins to draw these people to Himself at a pace appropriate for that particular individual. With the help of a spiritual guide, who does not force, but rather only suggests and clarifies matters for the aspirant, the novice Sufi begins the journey back to God by means of the instructions and techniques required for progress along the path. As the aspirant's will becomes ever-closer aligned with God's Will, it is the individual Sufi who freely chooses to progress further. There is no external force or pressure.

Sufism does not consist of obeying orders, submitting to a spiritual leader, engaging in constant self-criticism sessions, or employing various methods to "reform" or "cleanse" one's character or mind. It is not a "cult" in the current pejorative sense that this term has acquired in the West. Although these elements are present in Sufism, no one is predestined or commanded to engage in such activities. One cannot be coerced into following the Sufi path by threats or promises.

But, most important of all, Sufism is a life-long process of spiritual development. The reader will notice throughout this book that each stage or station is a gift from God. This does not mean, however, that the aspirant can sit back and wait for the gift to be bestowed. Quite the contrary: An individual must actively prepare himself or herself to receive the gift through the method set out by his or her spiritual guide. When the individual has accomplished this, the gift will be bestowed.

Secondly, the author emphasizes such concepts as spiritual poverty, helplessness, powerlessness, and yearning. These concepts have specific meanings in Sufism, all of which stem from the belief that God is the source of everything. For example, one cannot have true power because all power belongs to God. Therefore, in reality a person is powerless. One is helpless because there is no one who can provide assistance other than God. One's perception and admittance of helplessness and destitution before God, the source of everything, is the real source of a person's power and wealth. An individual is powerful by the Power of God, and wealthy by the Richness of God.

Understood in this context, one sees immediately that Sufism is a path demanding the individual's active participation in his or her spiritual growth and development. One is not allowed to be passive, hoping that God will bestow this or that blessing or station. Rather, one does what is necessary to grow spiritually, and God bestows the blessings and stations when the individual is ready to receive them.

Thirdly, in Islamic literature Prophet Muhammad's name is traditionally followed by a phrase calling God's blessings and peace upon him. In this book, we have chosen the phrase "upon him be peace and blessings." The reader will notice that the Prophet is not always mentioned by name, for the author refers to him by many titles: "the glory of humanity," "the lord of the penitents," "the best of creation," "the most truthful and confirmed one." The phrase that follows all of these titles, "upon him be peace and blessings" indicates that the author is referring to Prophet Muhammad.

Finally, we have added explanatory footnotes and made a conscious effort to make this translation gender-neutral, for every aspect of Islam applies to both men and women. This has not been done in cases of direct translations from the Qur'an, the *Hadith*, and classical sources, in order to maintain the integrity of the original Arabic. However, it should be understood that the masculine form, in *every* case when the reference is generalized, includes the female form as well. Islam is not a religion for men only, as is sometimes assumed by non-Muslims. Both sexes are equally responsible for their actions before God.

Sufism and Its Origin

Sufism (*tasawwuf*) is the path followed by Sufis to reach the Truth—God. While Sufism usually expresses the theoretical or philosophical aspect of this search, the practical aspect is usually referred to as "being a dervish."

like monastic order

What Is Sufism?

Sufism has been defined in many ways. Some see it as the annihilation of the individual's ego, will, and self centeredness by God and the subsequent spiritual revival with the light of His Essence[1]. Such a transformation results in the direction of the individual's will by God in accordance with His Will. Others view it as a continuous striving to cleanse one's self of all that is bad or evil in order to acquire virtue.

The definiton of Junayd al-Baghdadi, a famous Sufi master, gives the impression that he sees Sufism as a way of "self-annihilation in God" and "permanence or subsistence with God." Shibli summarizes it as always being together with God or in His presence, so that no worldly or other-worldly aim is even entertained. Abu Muhammad Jarir describes Sufism as resisting the temptations of the carnal, (evil-commanding) self (*nafs al-ammara*) and evil qualities, and acquiring laudable moral qualities.

There are some who describe Sufism as seeing behind the "outer" or surface appearance of things and events, and interpreting whatever happens in the world in relation to God. This means that a person regards every act of God as a window through which to "see" Him, and lives his life as a continuous effort to

---

[1] God's Essence (*Zat*) is the Divine Being Himself. The phrase "lights of His Essence" refers to the lights of His Being.

view or "see" Him with a profound, spiritual "seeing", indescribable in physical terms, and with a profound awareness of being continually overseen by Him.

All of these definitions can be summarized as follows: Sufism is the path followed by an individual who, having been able to free himself or herself from human vices and weaknesses in order to acquire angelic qualities and conduct pleasing to God, lives in accordance with the requirements of God's knowledge and love, and in the resulting spiritual delight that ensues.

Sufism is based on observing even the most "trivial" rules of the Shari'a[2] in order to penetrate their inner meaning. An initiate or traveler on the path (*salik*) never separates the outer observance of the Shari'a from its inner dimension, and therefore observes all of the requirements of both the outer and the inner dimensions of Islam. Through such observance, the traveler heads toward the goal in utmost humility and submission.

Sufism, a demanding path that leads to knowledge of God, has no room for negligence or frivolity. It requires the initiate to strive continuously, like a honeybee flying from hive to flowers and from flowers to hive, to acquire this knowledge. The initiate should purify his or her heart from all other attachments; resist all carnal inclinations, desires, and appetites; and live in a manner reflecting the knowledge with which God has revived and illumined his or her heart, always ready to receive divine blessing and inspiration; as well as in strict observance of Prophet Muhammad's example, upon him be peace and blessings. Convinced that attachment and adherence to God is the greatest merit and honor, the initiate should renounce his or her own desires for the demands of God, the Truth.

After these (preliminary) definitions, we should discuss the aim, benefits, and principles of Sufism.

---

[2] The body of Islamic law, based on the Qur'anic commands and the actions and sayings of the Prophet, upon him be peace and blessings, and then further developed by legal scholars to apply Islamic concepts to daily life.

Sufism requires the strict observance of all religious obligations, an austere lifestyle, and the renunciation of carnal desires. Through this method of spiritual self-discipline, the individual's heart is purified and his or her senses and faculties are employed in the way of God, which means that the traveler can now begin to live on a spiritual level.

Sufism also enables individuals, through the constant worship of God, to deepen their awareness of themselves as devotees of God. Through the renunciation of this transient, material world, as well as the desires and emotions it engenders, they awaken to the reality of the other world, which is turned toward the Beautiful Divine Names of God.[3] Sufism allows individuals to develop the moral dimension of one's existence, and enables the acquisition of a strong, heartfelt, and personally experienced conviction of the articles of faith that before had only been accepted superficially.

The principles of Sufism may be listed as follows:

· Reaching true belief in God's Divine Oneness and living in accordance with its demands.

· Heeding the Divine Speech (the Qur'an), discerning and then obeying the commands of the Divine Power and Will as they relate to the universe (the laws of creation and life).

· Overflowing with Divine Love and getting along with all other beings in the realization (originating from Divine Love) that the world is the cradle of brotherhood and sisterhood.

· Giving preference or precedence to the well-being and happiness of others.

---

[3] The world has three "faces." The first face is turned toward the transient, materialistic world, in which people seek the satisfaction of their bodily (animalistic) desires. The second face is turned toward the "arable field" of the Hereafter, in which a person's "seeds of action" are sown and, at the proper time, harvested in the Hereafter. The third face is the area in which the Beautiful Divine Names of God are manifested. Sufism requires the awakening to the last two "faces" of the world.

· Acting in accordance with the demands of the Divine Will—not with the demands of our own will—and living in a manner that reflects our self-annihilation in God and subsistence with Him.

· Being open to love, spiritual yearning, delight, and ecstasy.

· Being able to discern what is in the hearts or minds of others through facial expressions and the inner, Divine mysteries and the meanings of surface events.

· Visiting spiritual places and associating with people who encourage the avoidance of sin and striving in the way of God.

· Being content with religiously permitted pleasures, and not taking even a single step toward that which is not permitted.

· Struggling continuously against worldly ambitions and illusions, which lead us to believe that this world is eternal.

· Never forgetting that salvation is possible only through certainty of or conviction in the truth of religious beliefs and conduct, sincerity or purity of intention, and the sole desire to please God.

Two other elements may be added: acquiring knowledge and understanding of the religious and gnostic sciences, and following a perfected, spiritual master's guidance. Both of these are of considerable significance in the Naqshbandiyah Sufi order.

It may be useful to discuss Sufism according to the following basic concepts, which often form the core of books written on good morals, manners, and asceticism, and which are viewed as the sites of the "Muhammadan Truth"[4] in one's heart. They

---

[4] This term is essential to Sufism. It may be translated as the "reality of Muhammad" as God's Messenger, the most beloved of God, the best example for all creation to follow, the embodiment of Divine Mercy, and the living Qur'an or embodiment of the Qur'anic way of life.

can also be considered as lights by which to know and follow the spiritual path leading to God.

The first and foremost of these concepts is wakefulness (*yaqaza*), which is alluded to in the Prophetic saying (hadith): *My eyes sleep but my heart does not,* and in the saying of 'Ali, the fourth Caliph: *Men are asleep. They wake up when they die.* The many other stages on this path will be discussed, at some length, in this book.

The Origin of Sufism

As the history of Islamic religious sciences tells us, religious commandments were not written down during the early days of Islam; rather, the practice and oral circulation of commandments related to belief, worship, and daily life led the people to memorize them.

Thus it was easy to compile these in books later on, for what had been memorized and practiced was simply written down. In addition, since religious commandments were the vital issues in a Muslim's individual and collective life, scholars gave priority to these and compiled books. Legal scholars collected and codified books on Islamic law and its rules and principles pertaining to all fields of life. Traditionists[5] established the Prophetic traditions (*Hadith*s) and way of life (Sunna), and preserved them in books. Theologians dealt with issues concerning Muslim belief. Interpreters of the Qur'an dedicated themselves to studying its meaning, including issues that would later be called "Qur'anic sciences," such as *naskh* (abrogation of a law), *inzal* (God's sending down the entire Qur'an at one time), *tanzil* (God's sending down the Qur'an in parts on different occasions), *qira'at* (Qur'anic recitation), *ta'wil* (exegesis), and others.

---

[5] This term refers to scholars who have devoted themselves to the study of the *Hadith*s. Especially when used in the same sense as Sunna, the *Hadith*s are classified into three groups: The Prophet's words, his actions or daily life, and the sayings or actions of his Companions of which he approved explicitly or tacitly. They have been transmitted to succeeding generations through verified chains of narrators.

Thanks to these efforts that remain universally appreciated in the Muslim world, the truths and principles of Islam were established in such a way that their authenticity cannot be doubted.

While some scholars were engaged in these "outer" activities, Sufi masters were mostly concentrating on the pure spiritual dimension of the Muhammadan Truth. They sought to reveal the essence of humanity's being, the real nature of existence, and the inner dynamics of humanity and the cosmos by calling attention to the reality of that which lies beneath and beyond their outer dimension. Adding to Qur'anic commentaries, narrations of Traditionists, and deductions of legal scholars, Sufi masters developed their ways through asceticism, spirituality, and self-purification—in short, their practice and experience of religion.

Thus the Islamic spiritual life, based on asceticism, regular worship, abstention from all major and minor sins, sincerity and purity of intention, love and yearning, and the individual's admission of his or her essential impotence and destitution became the subject matter of Sufism, a new science possessing its own method, principles, rules, and terminology. Even if various differences gradually emerged among the orders that later were established, it can be said that the basic core of this science has always been the essence of the Muhammadan Truth.

The two aspects of the same truth—the commandments of the Shari'a and Sufism—have sometimes been presented as mutually exclusive. This is quite unfortunate, as Sufism is nothing more than the spirit of the Shari'a, which is made up of austerity, self-control and criticism, and the continuous struggle to resist the temptations of Satan and the evil-commanding self in order to fulfill religious obligations.[6] While adhering to the former has been regarded as exotericism (self-restriction to Islam's outer dimension), following the latter has been seen as pure esotericism. Although this discrimination arises partly from

---

[6] Sufism is based on the purification of the carnal self (*nafs*). The self needs to be trained and educated, for in its "raw" form it is evil. The Qur'an calls it *nafs ammara* (*bi al-su '*): the evil-commanding self.

assertions that the commandments of the Shari'a are represented by legal scholars or muftis, and the other by Sufis, it should be viewed more as the result of the natural, human tendency of assigning priority to that way which is most suitable for the individual practitioner.

Many legal scholars, Traditionists, and interpreters of the Qur'an produced important books based on the Qur'an and the Sunna. The Sufis, following methods dating back to the time of the Prophet and his Companions, also compiled books on austerity and spiritual struggle against carnal desires and temptations, as well as states and stations of the spirit. They also recorded their own spiritual experiences, love, ardor, and rapture. The goal of such literature was to attract the attention of those people who the Sufis regarded as having restricted their practice and reflection to the "outer" dimension of religion, and to direct their attention to the "inner" dimension of religious life.

Both Sufis and scholars sought to reach God by observing the Divine obligations and prohibitions. Nevertheless, some extremist attitudes—occasionally observed on both sides—caused disagreements. Actually, there was no substantial disagreement, and such conflicts should not have been viewed as disagreements, for they only involved dealing with different aspects and elements of religion under different titles. The tendency of specialists in jurisprudence to concern themselves with the rules of worship and daily life and how to regulate and discipline individual and social life, while Sufis chose to provide a way to live at a high level of spirituality through self-purification and spiritual training, cannot be considered a disagreement.

In fact, Sufism and jurisprudence are like the two colleges of a university that seeks to teach its students the two dimensions of the Shari'a, enabling them to practice it in their daily lives. One college cannot survive without the other, for while one teaches how to pray, be ritually pure, fast, give charity, and how to regulate all aspects of daily life, the other concentrates on what these and other actions really mean, how one can make worship an inseparable part of one's existence, and how to elevate each individual to the rank of a universal, perfect being (*al-insan al-kamil*)—a true human being.[7] That is why neither discipline can be neglected.

Although some self-proclaimed Sufis have labeled religious scholars as "scholars of ceremonies" and "exoterists", real, perfected Sufis have always depended on the basic principles of the Shari'a and have based their thoughts on the Qur'an and the Sunna. They have derived their methods from these basic sources of Islam. *Al-Wasaya wa al-Ri'aya* (The Advices and Observation of Rules) by al-Muhasibi, *Al-Ta'arruf li-Madhhab Ahl al-Sufi* (A Description of the Way of the People of Sufism) by Kalabazi, *Al-Luma'* (The Gleams) by al-Tusi, *Qut al-Qulub* (The Food of Hearts) by Abu Talib al-Makki, and *Al-Risala al-Qushayri* (The Treatise) by al-Qushayri are among the precious sources that discuss Sufism according to the Qur'an and the Sunna. Some of these sources concentrate on self-control and self-purification, while others elaborate upon various topics of concern to Sufis.

After these great compilers came Hujjat al-Islam Imam al-Ghazzali, author of *Ihya' al-'Ulum al-Din* (Reviving the Religious Sciences), his most celebrated work. He reviewed all of Sufism's terms, principles, and rules, and, establishing those that were agreed upon by all Sufi masters and criticizing others, united the outer (Shari'a and jurisprudence) and inner (Sufi) dimensions of Islam. Sufi masters who came after him presented Sufism as one of the religious sciences or a dimension thereof, promoting unity or agreement among themselves and the so-called "scholars of ceremonies." In addition, the Sufi masters made several Sufi subjects, such as the states of the spirit, certainty or conviction, sincerity and morality, part of the curriculum of *madrassas* (institutes for the study of religious sciences).

---

[7] This very famous Sufi term denotes an individual's final "spiritual" perfection, which causes him or her to have a universal "nature" that can represent the entire creation and reflect all that is best in it.

Although Sufism mostly concentrates on the individual's inner world and deals with the meaning and effect of the religious commandments on one's spirit and heart, and is therefore abstract, it does not contradict any of the Islamic ways based on the Qur'an and the Sunna. In fact, as is the case with other religious sciences, its source is the Qur'an and the Sunna, as well as the conclusions drawn from the Qur'an and the Sunna via *ijtihad* (deduction) by the verifying scholars of the early period of Islam. It dwells on knowledge, knowledge of God, certainty, sincerity, perfect goodness, and other similar, fundamental virtues.

Defining Sufism as the "science of esoteric truths or mysteries," or the "science of humanity's spiritual states and stations," or the "science of initiation" does not mean that it is completely different from other religious sciences. Such definitions have resulted from the Shari'a-rooted experiences of various individuals, all of whom have had different characters and dispositions, and who lived at different times.

It is a distortion to present the viewpoints of Sufis and the thoughts and conclusions of Shari'a scholars as essentially different from each other. Although some Sufis were fanatic adherents of their own ways, and some religious scholars (i.e., legal scholars, Traditionists, and interpreters of the Qur'an) did restrict themselves to the outer dimension of religion, those who follow and represent the middle, straight path have always formed the majority. Therefore, it is wrong to conclude that there is a serious disagreement (which most likely began with some unbecoming thoughts and words uttered by some legal scholars and Sufis against each other) between the two groups.

When compared with those who speak for tolerance and consensus, those who have started or participated in such conflicts are very few indeed. This is natural, for both groups have always depended on the Qur'an and the Sunna, the two main sources of Islam.

In addition, the priorities of Sufism have never been different from those of jurisprudence. Both disciplines stress the importance of belief and of engaging in good deeds and good conduct. The only difference is that Sufis emphasize self-purification, deepening the meaning of good deeds and multiplying them, and attaining higher moral standards so that one's conscience can awaken to the knowledge of God and thus embark upon a path that leads to the required sincerity in living Islam and obtaining God's good pleasure.[8]

By means of these virtues, men and women can acquire another nature, "another heart" (a spiritual intellect within the heart), a deeper knowledge of God, and another "tongue" with which to mention God. All of these will help them to observe the Shari'a commandments based on a deeper awareness of, and with a disposition for, devotion to God.

An individual practitioner of Sufism can use this system to deepen his or her spirituality. Through the struggle with one's self, solitude or retreat, invocation, self-control and self-criticism, the veils covering the inner dimension of existence are torn away, enabling the individual to acquire a strong conviction concerning the truth of all of Islam's major and minor principles.

Sofi or Sufi

Sofi is used to designate the followers of Sufism, particularly by speakers of Persian and Turkish. Others use the term Sufi. I think the difference most likely arises from the different views of the word's origin. Those who claim that it is derived from the word *sof* (wool), *safa* (spiritual delight, exhilaration), *safwat* (purity), or *sophos* (a Greek word meaning wisdom), or who believe that it implies devotion, prefer Sufi. Those who hold that it is derived from *suffa* (chamber), and stress that it should not be confused with *sofu* (religious zealot), also use Sufi.

The word *sufi* has been defined in many ways, among them:

---

[8] The phrase "God's (good) pleasure" means that God has accepted the action of His servant. It does not reflect emotion, and therefore does not resemble human pleasure.

· A traveler on the way to God who has purified his or her self and thus acquired inner light or spiritual enlightenment.

· A humble soldier of God who has been chosen by the Almighty for Himself and thus freed from the influence of his or her carnal, evil-commanding self.

· A traveler on the way to the Muhammadan Truth who wears a coarse, woolen cloak as a sign of humility and nothingness, and who renounces the world as the source of vice and carnal desire. Following the example of the Prophets and their followers, as well as sincere devotees, they are called *mutasawwif* to emphasize their spiritual states and belief, conduct, and life-style.

· A traveler to the peak of true humanity who has been freed from carnal turbidity and all kinds of human dirt to realize his or her essential, heavenly nature and identity.

· A spiritual person who tries to be like the people of the *Suffa*—the poor, scholarly Companions of the Prophet who lived in the chamber adjacent to the Prophet's Mosque—by dedicating his or her life to earning that name.

Some say that the word *sufi* is derived from *saf* (pure). Although their praiseworthy efforts to plase God by serving Him continually and keeping their hearts set on Him are enough for them to be called pure ones, such a derivation is grammatically incorrect. Some have argued that *sufi* is derived from *sophia* or *sophos*, Greek words meaning wisdom. I think this is a fabrication of foreign researchers who try to prove that Sufism has a foreign—and therefore non-Islamic—origin.

The first Muslim to be called a Sufi was the great ascetic Abu Hashim al-Kufi (d. 150 AH[9]). Thus, the word *sufi* was in use in the second Islamic century after the generation of the

---

[9] The Prophet's *hijra* (emigration to Madina) marks the beginning of the Muslim calendar. This event took place in July 16, 622 CE. As the Muslim calendar is lunar, it is shorter than its and solar counterpart.

Companions and their blessed successors. At this point in time, Sufism was characterized by spiritual people seeking to follow the footsteps of our Prophet, upon him be peace and blessings, and his Companions by imitating their life-styles. This is why Sufism has always been known and remembered as the spiritual dimension of the Islamic way of life.

Sufism seeks to educate people so that they will set their hearts on God and burn with love for Him. It focuses on high morals and proper conduct, as shown by the Prophets. Although some slight deviations may have appeared in Sufism over time, these should not be used to condemn that way of spiritual purity.

While describing Sufis who lead a purely spiritual life, Imam Qushayri writes:

> The greatest title in Islam is Companionship of the Prophet. This honor or blessing is so great that it can only be acquired by an actual Companion of the Prophet. The second rank in greatness belongs to the Tabi'un, those fortunate ones who came after the Companions and saw them. This is followed by the Taba'i al-Tabi'in, those who came after the Tabi'un and saw them. Just after the closing years of this third generation and coinciding with the outbreak of internal conflict and deviation in belief, and along with the Traditionists, legal scholars, and theologians who rendered great services to Islam, Sufis had great success in reviving the spiritual aspect of Islam.

Early Sufis were distinguished, saintly people who led upright, honest, austere, simple and blemish-free lives. They did not seek bodily happiness or carnal gratification, and followed the example of the Prophet. They were so balanced in their belief and thinking that they cannot be considered followers of ancient philosophers, Christian mystics, or Hindu holy men. Early Sufis considered Sufism as the science of humanity's inner world, the reality of things, and the mysteries of existence. A Sufi who studied this science was one determined to reach the final rank of a universal or perfect being.

Sufism is a long journey of unceasing effort leading to the Infinite One, a marathon to be run without stopping, with unyielding resolution, and without anticipating any worldly pleasure or reward. It has nothing to do with Western or Eastern mysticism, yoga, or philosophy, for a Sufi is a hero determined to reach the Infinite One, not a mystic, a yogi, or a philosopher.

Prior to Islam, some Hindu and Greek philosophers followed various ways leading to self-purification and struggled against their carnal desires and the attractions of the world. But Sufism is essentially different from these ways. For example, Sufis live their entire lives as a quest to purify their selves via invocation, regular worship, complete obedience to God, self-control, and humility, whereas ancient philosophers did not observe any of these rules or acts. Their self-purification—if it really deserves to be considered as such—was usually a source of creating conceit and arrogance in many of them, instead of humility and self-criticism.

Sufis can be divided into two categories: those who stress knowledge and seek to reach their destination through the knowledge of God (*ma'rifa*), and those who follow the path of yearning, spiritual ecstasy, and spiritual discovery.

Members of the first group spend their lives traveling toward God, progressing "in" and progressing "from" Him on the wings of knowledge and the knowledge of God. They seek to realize the meaning of: *There is no power and strength save with God*. Every change, alteration, transformation, and formation observed, and every event witnessed or experienced, is like a comprehensible message from the Holy Power and Will experienced in different tongues. Those in the second group also are serious in their journeying and asceticism. However, they may sometimes deviate from the main destination and fail to reach God Almighty, since they pursue hidden realities or truths, wonder-working, spiritual pleasure, and ecstasy. Although this path is grounded on the Qur'an and the Sunna, it may lead some initiates to cherish such desires and expectations as spiritual rank, the working of wonders, and sainthood. That is why the former path, which leads to the greatest sainthood under the guidance of the Qur'an, is safer.

Sufis divide people into three groups:

· *The perfect ones who have reached the destination.* This group is divided into two subgroups: the Prophets and the perfected ones who have reached the Truth by strictly following the prophetic examples. Not all perfected ones are guides; rather than guiding people to the Truth, some remain annihilated or drowned in the waves of the "ocean of meeting with God and amazement." As their relations with the visible, material world are completely severed, they cannot guide others.

· *The initiates.* This group also consists of two subgroups: those who completely renounce the world and, without considering the Hereafter, seek only God Almighty, and those who seek to enter Paradise, but do not give up tasting some of the world's permitted pleasures. Such people are known as ascetics, worshippers, the poor, or the helpless.

· *The settlers or clingers.* This group consists of people who only want to live an easy, comfortable life in this world. Thus, Sufis call them "settlers" or "clingers," for they "cling heavily to the earth." They are mainly people who do not believe, who indulge in sin and therefore cannot be pardoned. According to the Qur'an, they are unfortunate beings who belong to "the group on the left," or those who are "blind" and "deaf" and "without understanding."

Some have also referred to these three groups as the foremost (or those brought near to God), the people on the right, and the people on the left.[10]

---

[10] On the Day of Judgment, there will be two groups of people: those on the left side and those on the right side of God's Throne. The former did not believe in God and His Prophet, and led sinful lives. As they died without repenting, they will be judged worthy of entering Hell. The latter believed and sought to live according to the dictates and teachings of God, as revealed through His Prophets and Messengers. They repented and strove to obtain God's pleasure. They will be judged worthy of entering Paradise.

Tawba (Repentance), *Inaba* (Sincere Penitence), and *Awba* (Turning to God in Contrition)

Tawba (repentance) means that one feels regret and, filled with remorse for his or her sins, turns to God with the intention of obeying Him. According to truth-seeking scholars, repentance signifies a sincere effort to no longer oppose the Divine Essence in one's feelings, thoughts, intentions, and acts, and to comply sincerely with His commands and prohibitions. Repentance does not mean being disgusted with what is bad or prohibited and thus no longer engaging in it; rather, it means remaining aloof from whatever God hates and prohibits, even if it seems agreeable to sense and reason.

Repentance is usually modified by the adjective *nasuh* (i.e., The Qur'an, 66:8), literally meaning pure, sincere, reforming, improving, and repairing. *Tawba nasuh*—sincere, reforming, and improving repentance—means a pure, sincere repentance that perfectly reforms and improves the one who feels it. One who feels such a sincere, heartfelt, and true remorse for the sin committed seeks to abandon it, thereby setting a good example for others. The Qur'an points to this when it mentions true repentance: *O you who believe! Turn to God in true, sincere repentance* (66:8).

There are three categories of repentance:

· The repentance of those who cannot discern Divine truths. Such people are uneasy about their disobedience to God and, conscious of the sinfulness clouding their hearts, turn toward God in repentance saying, for example: *I have fallen or committed a sin. Forgive me,* or *I ask for God's forgiveness.*

· Those half-awakened to Divine truths beyond veils of material existence who feel an inward pang of sinfulness and remorse right after thinking or doing anything incompatible with the consciousness of always being in God's presence, or after every instance of heedlessness that envelops their hearts, and who immediately take refuge with the Mercy and Favor of God. Such people are described in the following Tradition:

> God's Messenger, upon him be peace and blessings, declared: *One who sincerely repents of his sin is as if he had never committed it. When God loves one of His servants, his sins do not harm him.* Then he recited the verse: *Assuredly, God loves the oft-repentant and those who always seek to purify themselves.* When asked about the sign of repentance, he declared: *It is heartfelt remorse.*[1]

· Those who live such a careful life that, as declared in a Tradition: *My eyes sleep but my heart does not,*[2] their hearts are awake. Such people immediately discard whatever intervenes between God and their hearts and other innermost faculties, and regain the consciousness of their relation to the Light of Lights. They always manifest the meaning of: *How excellent a servant! Truly he was ever turning in contrition (to his Lord)* (38:44).

Repentance means regaining one's essential purity after every spiritual defilement, and engaging in frequent self-renewal. The stages of repentance are:

· Feeling sincere remorse and regret

· Being frightened whenever one remembers past sins

· Trying to eradicate injustice and support justice and what is right

---

[1] Abu al-Qasim 'Abd al-Karim al-Qushayri, *Al-Risalat al Qushayriya fi 'Ulum al-Tasawwuf* (Cairo, 1972), 91.

[2] Muhammad ibn Isma'il al-Bukhari, "Tahajjud," in *Al-Jami' al-Sahih*, 4 vols. (Beirut, n.d.), 16; Abu al-Husayn Muslim ibn Hajjaj al-Qushayri Muslim, "Musafirin," in *Sahih al-Muslim*, 5 vols. (Beirut, 1956), 125.

· Reviewing one's responsibilities and performing previously neglected obligations

· Reforming oneself by removing spiritual defects caused by deviation and error

· Regretting and lamenting the times when one did not mention or remember God, or thank Him and reflect on His works. Such people are always apprehensive and alert in order that their thoughts and feelings are not tainted by things that intervene between themselves and God. (This last quality is particular to people distinguished by their nearness to God.)

If one does not feel remorse, regret, and disgust for errors committed, whether great or small; if one is not fearful or apprehensive of falling back into sin at any time; and if one does not take shelter in sincere servanthood to God in order to be freed from the deviation and error into which one has fallen by moving away from God, any resulting repentance will be no more than a lie.

On sincere penitence, the famous Sufi master Mawlana Jalal al-Din al-Rumi says:

> I have repented and turned to God so sincerely
> that I will not break [the vow of repentance] until my soul leaves my body.
> In fact, who other than an ass steps toward perdition
> after having suffered so much trouble (on account of his sins)?

Repentance is an oath of virtue, and holding steadfastly to it requires strong willpower. The lord of the penitents, upon him be peace and blessings, says that one who repents sincerely and holds steadfastly to it has achieved the rank of a martyr, while the repentance of those who cannot free themselves from their sins and deviations, although they repeatedly repent, mocks the "door" toward which the truly repentant ones turn in utmost sincerity and resolution.

One who continues to sin after proclaiming a fear of Hell, who does not engage in righteous deeds despite self-proclaimed desires for Paradise, and who is indifferent to the Prophet's way and practices despite assertions of love for the Prophet cannot be taken seriously. This is also the case with one who claims to be sincere and pure-hearted, but spends his or her life oscillating between sin and repentance.

An initiate's first station is repentance, while the second is *inaba* (sincere penitence). In common usage, *inaba* also refers to the ceremony that is held when one submits to a spiritual guide (as a *murshid*). While repentance requires the training of feelings, thoughts, and acts in order to move from opposition to acceptance and obedience, sincere penitence demands a critique of the authenticity, sincerity, and sufficiency of that acceptance and obedience. Repentance is a progression or journeying toward God—that is, seeking to do what is pleasing to God and refraining from what is forbidden by Him. Sincere penitence is an ascension through the stations of journeying in God—in other words, striving to live an upright life in self-annihilation and absorption in God so that one may seek His pleasure in all actions and thoughts.

Awba (turning to God in contrition) is an ascension through the stations of journeying from God—that is, being responsible for guiding others after having embodied the Islamic way of belief, thought, and conduct. In other words, taking refuge in God in fear of dying as a non-Muslim and deserving eternal punishment is repentance; annihilating one's self in God in the hope of preserving one's spiritual rank is sincere penitence; and closing one's self to any desires, ambitions, or aims other than God's good pleasure is turning to Him in utmost contrition.

The first is the state of all believers, and is expressed in: *Repent to God, O believers!* (24:31). The second is an attribute of saints and the foremost in belief and moral conduct who have been brought near God. Its beginning is seen in: *Turn to your Lord repentant* (39:54), and its end is stated in: *He comes with a contrite heart* (50:33). The third is for the Prophets and Messengers, all of whom are appreciated and praised by God in the words: *How excellent a servant! Truly he was ever turning in contrition* (*to his Lord*) (38:44).

The words of repentance uttered by those who are always conscious of being in the presence of God express the individual's sincere penitence or their turning to God in contrition. This is how the words of the best of creation, upon him be peace and blessings, should be understood when he said: *I ask God's forgiveness seventy* (*or one hundred,* according to another narration or version) *times a day.*

Repentance is the act or manner of those trying to live an upright life while remaining unaware of God's constant supervision of His servants and what nearness to Him really means. Those who live in awareness of God's nearness regard it as heedlessness to turn to God as ordinary people do, for He directs them as He wishes, constantly supervises them, and is nearer to them than anything else. Their station is not that of the people of the Unity of Being—ecstatic saints who view the creation while living in a state of being completely annihilated in God and therefore accept God as the only truly existent being. Rather, it is the station of the people of the Unity of the Witnessed— scholarly saints who accept that the truly existent one is He Who is witnessed or discerned beyond the creation. More than that, it is the station of those progressing in the light of Prophet Muhammad's practice, upon him be peace and blessings.

It is merely an assertion and a groundless claim when those who have not attained this station, and thus live [merely] on the outer surface of their existence, talk of *awba* and *inaba,* and especially of the final points of these two stations.

Muhasaba (Self-Criticism or Self-Interrogation)

Muhasaba literally means reckoning, settling accounts, and self-interrogation. In a spiritual context, however, it takes on the additional meaning of the self-criticism of a believer who constantly analyzes his or her deeds and thoughts in the hope that correcting them will bring him or her closer to God. Such a believer thanks God for the good he or she has done, and tries to erase his or her sins and deviations by imploring God for forgiveness and amending his or her errors and sins through repentance and remorse. *Muhasaba* is a very important and serious attempt to assert one's personal loyalty to God.

It is recorded by Muhy al-Din ibn al-'Arabi, author of *al-Futuhat al-Makkiya* (The Makkan Conquests), that during the early centuries of Islam, righteous people would either write down or memorize their daily actions, thoughts, and words, and then analyze and criticize themselves for any evil or sin they had committed. They did this to protect themselves from the storms of vanity and the whirls of self-pride. They would ask God's forgiveness after this self-analysis, and would repent sincerely so that they might be protected against future error and deviation. Then they would prostrate in thankfulness to God for the meritorious deeds or words that the Almighty had created through them.

Self-criticism may also be described as seeking and discovering one's inner and spiritual depth, and exerting the necessary spiritual and intellectual effort to acquire true human values and develop the sentiments that encourage and nourish them. This is how one distinguishes between good and bad, beneficial and harmful, and how one maintains an upright heart. Furthermore, it enables a believer to evaluate the present and prepare for the future. Again, self-criticism enables a believer to make amends for past mistakes and be absolved in the sight of God, for it provides a constant realization of self-renewal in one's inner world. Such a condition enables one to achieve a steady relationship with God, for this relationship depends on a believer's ability to live a spiritual life and remain aware of what takes place in his or her inner world. Success results in the preservation of one's celestial nature as a true human being, as well as the continual regeneration of one's inner senses and feelings.

A believer, in his or her spiritual and daily life, cannot be indifferent to self-criticism. On the one hand, he or she tries to revive his or her ruined past with the breezes of hope and mercy, blown by such Divine calls as: *Repent to God* (24:31) and: *Turn to Your Lord repentant* (39:54), which come from the worlds beyond and echo in his or her conscience. On the other hand, warnings as frightening as thunderbolts and as exhilarating as mercy and contained in such verses as: *O you who believe! Fear God and observe your duty to Him. And let every soul consider what it has prepared for the morrow* (59:18), bring the believer to his or her senses and make him or her alert once again against committing new sins. In such a condition, a believer is defended against all kinds of evil, as if enclosed behind locked doors.

Taking each moment of life to be a time of germination in spring, a believer seeks ever-greater depths in his or her spirit and heart with insight and consciousness arising from belief. Even if a believer is sometimes pulled down by the carnal dimension of his or her being and falters, he or she is always on the alert, as stated in: *Those who fear God and observe His commandments, when a passing stroke from Satan troubles them, they immediately remember (God), and lo! they are all aware* (7:201).

Self-criticism resembles a lamp in the heart of a believer, a warner and a well-wishing adviser in his or her conscience. Every believer uses it to distinguish between what is good and evil, beautiful and ugly, pleasing and displeasing to God. Through the guidance of this well-wishing adviser, the believer surmounts all obstacles, however seemingly insurmountable, and reaches the desired destination.

Self-criticism attracts Divine mercy and favor, which enables one to go deeper in belief and servanthood, to succeed in practicing Islam, and to attain nearness to God and eternal happiness. It also prevents one from falling into despair, which will ultimately lead to reliance on personal acts of worship to be saved from Divine punishment in the Hereafter.[3]

As self-criticism opens the door to spiritual peace and tranquillity, it also causes one to fear God and His punishment. In the hearts of those who constantly criticize themselves and call themselves to account for their deeds, this Prophetic warning is always echoed: *If you knew what I know, you would laugh little but weep much.*[4] Self-criticism, which gives rise to both peacefulness and fear in one's heart, continuously inspires anxiety in the hearts of those who are fully aware of the heavy responsibility they feel—the anxiety such as that which is voiced in: *If only I had been a tree cut into pieces.*[5]

Self-criticism causes the believer to always feel the distress and fear expressed in: The *earth seemed constrained to them for all its vastness, and their own souls straitened to them* (9:118). The verse: *Whether you make known what is in your souls or hide it, God will bring you to account for it* (2:284) resounds in

---

[3] If one despairs (of Divine mercy) concerning his or her eternal life because of his or her sins, relief from Divine punishment is sought. Such a person then remembers and relies on past good deeds. However, this way is utterly inadequate, for only through Divine mercy can one be saved from God's punishment and enter Paradise.

[4] Al-Bukhari, "Kusuf," 2; Muslim, "Salat," 112; Abu 'Isa Muhammad ibn 'Isa al-Tirmidhi, "Kusuf," in *Sunan*, 4 vols. (Beirut, n.d.), 2.

[5] Al-Tirmidhi, "Zuhd," 9; Muhammad ibn Yazid al-Qazwini Ibn Maja, "Zuhd," in *Sunan*, 2 vols. (Egypt, 1952), 19.

every cell of their brains, and they groan with utterances like: *I wish my mother had not given birth to me!*[6]

While it is difficult for everyone to achieve this degree of self-criticism, it is also difficult for those who do not do so to be sure that they will be able to live today better than yesterday, and tomorrow better than today. Those who are crushed between the wheels of time, whose current day is not better than the preceding one, cannot perform their duties pertaining to the afterlife well.

Constant self-criticism and self-reprimand show the perfection of one's belief. Everyone who has planned his or her life to reach the horizon of a perfect, universal human being is conscious of this life and spends every moment of it struggling with themselves. Such a person demands a password from whatever occurs to his or her heart and mind. Self-control against the temptations of Satan or the excitement of temper are practiced, and words and actions are carefully watched. Self-criticism is constant, even for those acts that seem most sensible and acceptable. Evening reviews of words and actions said or done during the day are the rule, as are morning resolutions to avoid sins. A believer knits the "lace of his or her life" with the "threads" of self-criticism and self-accusation.[7]

So long as a believer shows such loyalty and faithfulness to the Lord and lives in such humility, the doors of heaven will be thrown open and an invitation will be extended: *Come, O faithful one. You have intimacy with Us. This is the station of intimacy. We have found you a faithful one.* Every day he or she is honored with a new, heavenly journey in the spirit. It is God Himself Who swears by such a purified soul in: *Nay, I swear by the self-accusing soul!* (75:2).

---

[6] Muhammad Ibn Sa'd, *Al Tabaqat al-Kubra*, 8 vols. (Beirut, 1980), 3:360.

[7] In other words, all moments of one's life are spent in self-criticism and constant awareness of what one says and does.

Tafakkur (Reflection)

Tafakkur literally means to think on a subject deeply, systematically, and in great detail. In this context, it signifies reflection, which is the heart's lamp, the soul's food, the spirit of knowledge, and the essence and light of the Islamic way of life. Reflection is the light in the heart that allows the believer to discern what is good and evil, beneficial and harmful, beautiful and ugly. Again, it is through reflection that the universe becomes a book to study, and the verses of the Qur'an disclose their deeper meanings and secrets more clearly. Without reflection, the heart is darkened, the spirit is exasperated, and Islam is lived at such a superficial level that it is devoid of meaning and profundity.

Reflection is a vital step in becoming aware of what is going on around us and of being able to draw conclusions from these events. It is a golden key that opens the door of experience, the seedbed where the trees of truth are planted, and the opening of the heart's eye. Due to this, the greatest representative of humanity, the foremost in reflection and all other virtues, upon him be peace and blessings, states: *No act of worship is as meritorious as reflection. So reflect on God's bounties and the works of His Power, but do not try to reflect on His Essence, for you will never be able to do that.*[8] With these words, in addition to pointing out the merit of reflection, the glory of mankind, upon him be peace and blessings, determines the limits of reflection and reminds us of our limits.

In order to draw attention to the same point, the writer of *Al-Minhaj* (The Way Traced) writes:

---

[8] Abu Bakr Muhammad ibn Husayn al-Bayhaqi, "Shu'ab al-Iman," in *Kitab al-Sunan al-Kabir*, 9 vols. (Beirut, 1990), 1:136; Isma'il ibn Muhammad al-'Ajluni, *Kashf al-Khafa' wa Muzil al-Ilbas*, 2 vols. (Beirut 1351 AH / 1932 CE), 1:311.

Reflection on bounties is a condition of following this way,
While reflection on the Divine Essence is a manifest sin.
It is both false and useless to doubt and think about Him,
And also means seeking to obtain something already obtained.

The verse: *They reflect on the creation of the heavens and Earth* (3:190) presents the book of the universe with its creation, the peculiarities of its letters and words, the harmony and coherence of its sentences, and its firmness as a whole. By drawing our attention to the universe and calling us to reflect upon it, the Qur'an shows us one of the most beneficial methods of reflection: to reflect on and study the Qur'an, and to follow it in all our thoughts and actions; to discover the Divine mysteries in the book of the universe and, through every new discovery that helps the true believer deepen and unfold his or her reflections to live a life full of spiritual pleasure along a way of light extending from belief to knowledge of God and therefrom to love of God; and then to progress to the Hereafter and God's good pleasure and approval—this is the way to become a perfect, universal human being.

One can use reflection in every scientific field. However, the rational and experimental sciences are only a first step or a means to reach the final target of reflection, which is knowledge of God, provided that one's mind has not been filled with incorrect conceptions and premises. Studying existence as if it were a book to be reflected upon can engender the desired results and provide ceaseless information and inspiration, but only if one admits that all things and their attributes are created by God. This is what is sought and should be done by those who attribute all things to God, and who have attained spiritual contentment through the knowledge, love, and remembrance of God.

Reflection must be based on and start with belief in God as the Originator of creation. If not, one might reach God at some stage of the journey, but will not progress beyond the conviction of God's Existence and Unity. Reflection based on and starting with belief in God as the Creator and unique Administrator of all creation enables continuous progression and increased depths, for new discoveries develop into further dimensions (love of God, "annihilation in and subsistence with God," discovering Divine realities behind things and events). In other words, reflection, starting with awareness of God having the Names of "the First" and "the Outer" and progressing toward Him as "the Last" and "the Inner," will enable one to progress uninterruptedly and without end. Encouraging people to engage in reflection focused upon a determined aim entails urging them to learn and use the methods of sciences that study how existence is manifested.

Since everything in the heavens and Earth is the property and kingdom of God, studying every incident, item, and quality also means studying how the exalted Creator deals with existence. The believer who studies and accurately comprehends this book of existence, and then designs his or her life accordingly, will follow the way of guidance and righteousness to the final station of Paradise, where he or she will drink of *kawthar*—the blessed water of Paradise.

The people of loss and perdition wander in the pits of heedlessness and ingratitude to God, the true Owner of the infinite variety of beauty and bounty in the world; those following the way to Paradise, and equipped with reflection, recognize the True Giver of all bounty and obey Him, fully conscious of what believing in Him means. They travel from gratitude to being provided with all bounties, and from bounty to gratitude, in the footsteps of the angels, the Prophets, and the truthful and loyal believers, seeking God's pleasure in order to thank Him for His blessings. Using the vehicle of reflection and with the help of remembering God, they surmount all obstacles and, progressing from taking necessary measures to attain their goal, to submission, and from submission to committing their affairs to the Power of God, they fly through the heavens to their final destinations.[9]

---

[9] There are numerous final destinations. Some of them are entering Paradise, obtaining God's pleasure, and being rewarded with His vision.

Firar and *I'tisam* (Fleeing and Taking Shelter)

Firar, which literally means to run away from something, is used in Sufism to denote the journey from the created to the Creator, sheltering from the "shadow" in the "original,"[10] and renouncing the "drop" of water in order to plunge into the "ocean."[11] Further, it means discontent with the piece of glass (in which the Sun is reflected) and the turning to the "Sun,"[12] thereby escaping the confinement of self-adoration to "melt away" in the rays of the Truth. The verse *flee to God* (51:50), which points to a believer's journeying in heart and in spirit, refers to this action of the heart, the spiritual intellect.

The more distant people are from the suffocating atmosphere of corporeality and the carnal dimension, the nearer they are to God, and the more respect they have for themselves. Let us hear from Prophet Moses, upon him be peace, a loyal devotee at the door of the Truth, how one fleeing to and taking shelter in God is rewarded: *Then I fled from you [Pharaoh] when I feared you, and my Lord has granted to me the power of judging (justly and distinguishing between truth and falsehood, and right and wrong) and has made me one of His Messengers* (26:21). Prophet Moses states that the way to spiritual pleasure and meeting with God, the Divine vicegerency and nearness to Him goes through a stage of fleeing.

---

[10] Sufis view the creation as a shadow of the original, the meaning, the origin, in the Knowledge of God.

[11] Sufis consider everything in the world as being no more than a drop, maybe even a mirage, of the ocean. Material existence and pleasures are regarded as having the meaning and worth of a drop of water, while the other world and spiritual pleasures coming from Divine knowledge and love correspond to an ocean.

[12] The piece of glass signifies Divine manifestations in the world, while the Sun signifies God, the Origin of these manifestations.

Ordinary people flee from life's tumults and sin's ugliness to take refuge in God's forgiveness and favor. They declare or consider the meaning of: *My Lord, forgive and have compassion, for You are the Best of the Compassionate* (23:118). They seek God's shelter in total sincerity, saying: *I take refuge in You from the evil of what I have done.*[13]

Those distinguished by their piety and nearness to God flee from their own lesser qualities to the Divine Attributes, from feeling with their outward senses to discerning and observing with the heart, from ceremonial worship to its innermost dimension, and from carnal feelings to spiritual sensations. This is what is referred to in: *O God, I take refuge in Your approval from Your wrath, and in Your forgiveness from Your chastisement.*[14]

The most advanced in knowledge and love of God and in piety flee from Attributes to the Divine Being or Essence, and from the Truth to the Truth Himself. They say: *I take refuge in You from You,*[15] and are always in awe of God.

All who flee seek shelter and protection. As the consciousness of fleeing is proportionate to the spiritual profundity of the one fleeing, the quality of the destination reached varies according to the degree of the seeker's awareness. Members of the first group arrive at knowledge of God. They remember God in everything they see, mention Him, cherish desires, imagine things that are impossible for them to realize, and finally come to rest at sensing the reality of: *We have not been able to know You as knowing You requires, O Known One.* They always feel and repeat in ecstasy:

> Beings are in pursuit of knowledge of You,
> And those who attempt to describe You are unable to do so.
> Accept our repentance, for we are human beings
> Unable to know You as knowing You requires.

---

[13] Al-Tirmidhi, "Dawa'at," 15; Abu 'Abd al-Rahman ibn Shu'ayb al-Nasa'i, "Isti'adha," in *Sunan al-Nasa'i*, 8 vols. (Beirut, 1930), 57.

[14] *Muslim*, "Salat," 222.

[15] Ibid.

Members of the second group sail every day for a new ocean of knowing God, and spend their lives in ever-renewed glow of Divine manifestation. However, they cannot be saved from the obstacles that block them from the final station, where their overflowing spirit will subside. With their eyes fixed on the steps of the stairway that leads to higher and higher ranks, they fly upward from one rank to another; however, they also tremble with the fear that they might descend. Members of the third group, freed from the tides of the state (see the chapter: *Hal and Maqam*) and drowned in amazement (see the chapter: *Dahsha and Hayra*), are so intoxicated with the "wine coming from the source of everything" that even the Trumpet of Israfil[16] cannot cause them to recover from that stupor. Only one who has reached this rank can describe the profundity of their thoughts and feelings. Rumi says:

> Those illusions are traps for saints, whereas in reality
> They are the reflections of those with radiant faces in the garden of God.[17]

The "garden of God" signifies the manifestation of Divine Unity—the manifestations of one, many, or all the Divine Names throughout the universe. "Those with radiant faces" denotes the Divine Names and Attributes focused on a single thing or being. So, the meaning of the couplet is this: The traps in which saints are caught are the manifestations of the Divine Names and Attributes. These manifestations consist of the illusions in the viewof those blind to Divine truths. In the words of Sari Abdullah Efendi, the hearts of the Prophets and saints are mirrors that reflect the Names and Attributes of God. God also manifests His Names and Attributes as the Lord—Ruler, Sustainer, and Master—of the universe, making it a garden with ever-renewed beauties and charms that enrapture the Prophet and the saints.

---

[16] Israfil is one of the four archangels. He will blow the trumpet just before the end of the universe. This may be metaphorical.

[17] Mawlana Jalal al-Din al-Rumi, *Al-Mathnawi al-Kabir*, 6 vols. (Istanbul, n.d.), 1:3.

Halwat and *'Uzlat* (Privacy and Seclusion)

Literally meaning solitude and living alone, *halwat* and *'uzlat* (privacy and seclusion) within the context of Sufism denote an initiate's going into retreat to dedicate all of his or her time to worshipping God under the guidance and supervision of a spiritual master. He or she seeks purification from all false beliefs, dark thoughts and feelings, and conceptions and imaginations that separate him or her from the Truth, closing the doors of his or her heart to all that is not God, and conversing with Him through the tongue of his or her inner faculties.

Seclusion is one dimension of privacy; austerity is another. The first step in privacy is completed in forty days, therefore known as the forty-day period of austerity. When the spiritual master takes the initiate into privacy, he takes him or her to a quiet room, where he prays for the initiate's success, and then leaves. In that room, the initiate lives an austere life, utterly alone. He or she eats and drinks little in that room of seclusion, which is regarded as a door opening on nearness to God. Bodily needs decrease and are disciplined, carnal desires are forgotten, and all time is dedicated to worshipping God, meditation, reflection, prayer, and supplication.

In its aspect of the avoidance of people and austerity, privacy dates back to the early days of Sufism, even to the great Prophets. Numerous Prophets and saints, most particularly the glory of humankind, upon him be peace and blessings, spent portions of their lives in seclusion. However, their original system of privacy and seclusion has undergone undesirable change over time. The seclusion of Prophet Abraham, the forty-day periods of Prophet Moses, the austerity of Prophet Jesus, and the privacy of the prince of the Prophets have been practiced in different ways by many people, and have therefore undergone certain alterations.

Such changes can be regarded as natural to some extent, for in as much as seclusion is related to an individual's moods, temperament, and spiritual capacity, only perfect spiritual masters can know and decide how long and under what conditions an initiate must be kept in seclusion. In the early days of his initiation, Rumi underwent many forty-day periods of austerity in seclusion. However, when he found a true, perfect master, he left seclusion for the company of people (*jalwat*). Many others before and after him have preferred being with people, rather than avoiding them.

Austerity, one of the two dimensions of privacy, means keeping a tight rein on carnal gratification and urging the spirit to rise to human perfection, with which it is enamored.[18] Only through austerity can the carnal self be restrained, forced to renounce evil impulses and passions and submit to the commandments of God, forced to adopt humility and be the soil of a flowerbed:

> Be like earth so that roses may grow in you
> For nothing other than soil can be a medium for the growth of roses.

One can receive a certain Divine grace through austerity. Some can adorn their knowledge with high morals and their religious acts with sincerity and pure intention, thereby gaining mannerliness in their relations with both God and people. Others find themselves tossed this way and that in their relationship with their Lord, and continuously search for ways to get nearer to Him. There are still others who, like a moth just out of its cocoon, spend their lives among spiritual beings who may be regarded as the butterflies of the celestial worlds they have just reached.

---

[18] As the spirit is from God, it innately longs for Him and is enamored with perfection. The carnal soul or self, on the other hand, is enamored with animal desires.

What is essential to privacy is that the initiate must seek nothing other than God's pleasure, and must constantly wait in expectation of that Divine favor. The initiate must not be idle while waiting for this favor, but rather wait with the eye of his or her heart open, in the utmost care and excitement, so that no Divine inspiration or gift that may flow into his or her heart will be missed. They must wait with the courtesy and decorum appropriate to being in the presence of God. The following words of La Makani Husain Efendi express this meaning very aptly:

> Clean the fountain of your soul until it becomes perfectly pure.
> Fix your eyes on your heart until your heart becomes an eye.
> Give up doubts and put the pitcher of your heart to that fountain.
> When that pitcher is filled with the water which gives delight,
> Withdraw yourself and submit to its Owner His home.[19]
> When you leave it, God doubtless comes to His home.
> Never let the devil-robber enter the home of your heart,
> For once he has entered, it is very difficult to throw him out.

It is true that God is absolutely free of all time and space constraints, and that His relationship with the believer occurs on the "slopes" of the believer's heart. For this reason, the heart's "emerald hills" or "slopes" must always be ready to receive the waves of His manifestations so that, in the words of Ibrahim Haqqi of Erzurum, *the King may descend to His palace at night.*

God Almighty decreed to Prophet David: *Keep that home empty for Me so that I will be in it.*[20] Some have interpreted "keeping the heart empty" as purifying the heart of all that is not God, and as not having relations with others without first considering God's pleasure. The following words of Rumi express this most appropriately:

> One wise and sensible prefers the bottom of the well,
> For the soul finds delight in privacy (to be with God).
> The darkness of the well is preferable to the darkness people cause.

---

[19] "Home" signifies the heart, whose Owner is God.

[20] Al-Qushayri, *Al-Risala*, 327.

One holding on to the legs of people has never been able to arrive with a head.[21]
One must seclude oneself from others, not from the Beloved.
Fur is worn in winter, not in spring.

Since the purpose of seclusion is to purify the heart of the love which is not directed toward God and to be always with the Beloved, those who always feel the presence of God while living among people and who continuously discern the Divine Unity amidst multiplicity are regarded as always being with God in seclusion. In contrast, however, the seclusion of others who, although they spend their lives in seclusion, have not purified their hearts from attachment to whatever is other than God, is a deception.

Those who always feel themselves in the presence of God do not need to seclude themselves from people. Such people, in the words of Rumi, are like those who keep one foot in the sphere of Divine commandments and turn the other, like a compass needle, round the world. They experience ascent and descent at every moment. This is the seclusion recognized and preferred by the Prophets and saints.

God Almighty once said to Prophet David: *O David, why do you seclude yourself from people and choose to remain alone?* David, upon him be peace, answered: *Lord, I renounce the company of people for Your sake.* The Almighty warned him: *Always keep vigil, but do not keep aloof from your brethren. However, seclude yourself from those whose company is of no benefit to you.*

---

[21] That is, one who relies on people to attain his or her goal will fail.

Hal and *Maqam* (State and Station)

Hal (state) denotes experiencing in one's inner world the "breaths" blowing from the realms beyond the world, and feeling the difference between the "night" and "day," as well as the "evening" and "morning," that occur to the heart. Those who understand these as alternate waves of rejoicing and grief and of contraction and expansion invading the heart without the believer making a special effort, call the stable continuation of those waves "station" and their disappearance "sensuality."

It would not be wrong to describe each state as a Divine gift and the breeze of nearness to God one feels in the heart, and each station as one's continuous and stable experience of this breeze and the acquisition of a second nature. Like life, light, and mercy, each state is a direct gift of the Almighty and leads to the conviction of Divine Unity. By contrast, since each station depends on a purposeful effort, it cannot reflect the truth so manifestly. Therefore, without viewing stations as being obtained by a personal effort, a believer's feeling of the spiritual occurences in his or her heart, and a believer's opening a new way in his or her heart to the One known by the heart at every moment, results in a deeper appreciation of the Source of those occurrences than would be possible by shaping them according to one's own capacity and character, which may lead to ostentation and conceit.

The most truthful and confirmed one, upon him be peace and blessings, once declared: *God considers not your bodily statures, but your hearts.*[22] These words direct our attention to what is important for the Truth, and show people how to reach the main target. The Tradition narrated

---

[22] Muslim, "Birr," 33, 34.

through a less reliable channel is: *God considers your hearts and actions.*[23] This is a reference to a station reached after cycles of state.

A state consists of Divine manifestations occurring at times determined by the absolute Will. These manifestations are reflected in the heart and in the believer's perception and consciousness, which pursue and cast them into a mold. For this reason, while a station signifies stability and subsidence after waves of state, a state can be likened to groups of waves of different lengths and colors coming from the Sun, appearing and then disappearing, being dependent on the absolutely dominant Will.

Sensitive souls and those whose consciousness is alert or awakened to the knowledge of God discern the waves of state upon their hearts, just as they see the Sun's reflections on water, and respond to these waves according to their level and manner of perception. Those who have not corrected the imbalance of their hearts, and thus live disconnected from the Almighty, may regard these waves of state as illusions and fancies, while those who see existence with the light of the Truth view them as manifest, experienced realities.

The greatest hero of state, upon him be peace and blessings, who regarded each spiritual gift received as less when compared to the one that followed—may God illuminate our hearts with the light of his gifts he regarded as less—declared: *I ask God's forgiveness seventy times a day.*[24] It was impossible for a perfectly pure soul who felt the need for an everlasting mount and an eternal light in a never-ending journey toward the Infinite Being to have done otherwise.

---

[23] Ibid.; Ibn Maja, "Zuhd," 9.

[24] Al-Bukhari, "Dawa'at," 3; Al-Tirmidhi, "Tafsir al-Qur'an," 47.

Qalb (Heart) - 1

In the words of Ibrahim Haqqi of Erzurum:

The heart is the home of God; purify it from whatever is other than Him
So that the All-Merciful may descend into His palace at night.

The word *"Qalb"* (heart) has two meanings. One denotes the body's most vital organ, which is located on the left side of the chest. With respect to its structure and tissue, the heart is different from all other bodily parts: it has two auricles and two ventricles, is the origin of all arteries and veins, works by itself, like a motor, and, like a suction pump, moves blood through the system.

In Sufi terminology, the spiritual heart is the center of all emotions and (intellectual and spiritual) faculties, such as perception, consciousness, the senses, reasoning, and willpower. Sufis call it the "human truth"; philosophers call it the "speaking selfhood." An individual's real nature is found in the heart. With respect to this intellectual and spiritual aspect of existence, one is able to know, perceive, and understand. Spirit is the essence and inner dimension of this faculty; the biological spirit or the soul is its mount.

It is one's heart that God addresses and it is this that undertakes responsibilities, suffers punishment or is rewarded, is elevated through true guidance or debased through deviation, and is honored or humiliated. The heart is also the "polished mirror" in which Divine knowledge is reflected.

The heart both perceives and is perceived. The believer uses it to penetrate his or her soul, corporeal existence and mind, for it is like the eye of the spirit. Insight may be regarded as its faculty of sight, reason as its spirit, and will as its inner dynamics.

The heart or spiritual intellect, if we may so call it, has an intrinsic connection with its biological counterpart. The nature of this connection has been discussed by philosophers and Muslim sages for centuries. Of whatever nature this connection may be, it is beyond doubt that there is a close connection between the biological heart and the "spiritual" one, which is a Divine faculty, the center of true humanity, and the source of all human feelings and emotions.

In the Qur'an, religious sciences, morals, literature, and Sufism, the word "heart" signifies the spiritual heart. Belief, knowledge and love of God, and spiritual delight are the objectives to be won through this Divine faculty. The heart is a luminous, precious ore with two aspects, one looking to the spiritual world and the other to the corporeal, material world. If an individual's corporeal existence or physical body is directed by the spirit, the heart conveys to the body the spiritual effusions or the gifts it receives through the world of the spirit, and enables the body to breathe with peace and tranquillity.

As stated above, God considers one's heart. He treats men and women according to the quality of their hearts, as the heart is the stronghold of many elements vital to the believer's spiritual life and humanity: reason, knowledge, knowledge of God, intention, belief, wisdom, and nearness to God Almighty. If the heart is alive, all of these elements and faculties are alive; if the heart is diseased, it is difficult for the elements and faculties mentioned to remain sound. The truthful and confirmed one, upon him be peace and blessings, declared: *There is a fleshy part in the body. If it is healthy, then the whole of the body is healthy. If it is corrupted, then all the body is corrupted. Beware! That part is the heart.*[25] This saying shows the importance of the heart for one's spiritual health.

The heart has another aspect or function, one that is actually more important than those already mentioned: The heart has

---

[25] Al-Bukhari, "Iman," 39; Muslim, "Musaqat," 107.

points of reliance and the seeking of help ingrained in it, as well as in human nature, by which the heart enables the individual to perceive God as the All-Helping and All-Maintaining. That is, the heart always reminds one of God in terms of need, seeking help and protection. This is vividly expressed in a narrated Prophetic Tradition, which Ibrahim Haqqi relates as follows:

> God said: "Neither the heavens nor the earth can contain Me."
> He is known and recognized as a "Treasure" hidden
> in the heart by the heart itself.

The individual's body is the physical dimension of his or her existence, while one's heart constitutes its spiritual dimension. For this reason, the heart is the direct, eloquent, most articulate, splendid, and truthful tongue of the knowledge of God. Therefore, it is regarded as more valuable and honored than the Ka'ba, and accepted as the only exponent of the sublime truth expressed by the whole of creation to make God known.

The heart also is a fortress in which one can maintain sound reasoning and thinking, as well as a healthy spirit and body. As all human feelings and emotions take shelter and seek protection in this fortress, the heart must be protected and kept safe from infection. If the heart is infected, it will be very difficult to restore it; if it dies, it is almost impossible to revive it. The Qur'an, by advising us to pray: *Our Lord! Do not cause our hearts to swerve after You have guided us* (3:7), and our master, upon him be peace and blessings, by his supplication: *O God, O Converter of hearts! Establish our hearts firmly on Your religion,*[26] remind us of the absolute need to preserve the heart.

Just as the heart can function as a bridge by which all good and blessings may reach the believer, it can also become a means by which Satanic and carnal temptations and vices can enter. When set on God and guided by Him, the heart resembles a projector that diffuses light to even the furthest, remotest, and

---

[26] Al-Tirmidhi, "Qadar," 7; Ahmad Ibn Hanbal, *Musnad*, 6 vols. (Beirut, 1969), 6:302.

darkest corners of the body. If it is commanded by the (inherently evil) self, it can become a target for Satan's poisonous arrows. The heart is the native home of belief, worship, and perfect virtue; a river gushing with inspiration and radiation arising from the relationships among God, humanity, and the universe. Unfortunately, innumerable adversaries seek to destroy this home, to block this river or divert its course: hardness of heart (losing the ability to feel and believe), unbelief, conceit, arrogance, worldly ambition, greed, excessive lust, heedlessness, selfishness, and attachment to status.

Qalb (Heart) - 2

Belief is the life of the heart; worship is the blood flowing in its veins; and reflection, self-supervision, and self-criticism are the foundations of its permanence. The heart of an unbeliever is dead; the heart of a believer who does not worship is dying; and the heart of a believer who worships but does not engage in self-reflection, self-control, or self-criticism is exposed to many spiritual dangers and diseases.

The first group of people carry a "pump" in their chests, but it cannot be said that they have hearts. The second group of people live in the cloudy, misty atmosphere of their surmises and doubts, separate from God, and are unable to reach their destination. The third group of people, those who have traveled some distance toward the destination, are at risk because they have not yet reached the goal. They advance falteringly, struggling on the way of God, experience cycles of defeat and success, and spend their lives trying to climb a "hill" without being able to reach the summit.

On the other hand, those who have a firm belief live as if they see God and in the consciousness that God sees them, enjoy complete security and are under God's protection. They study existence with insight, penetrate the nature of existence, discover their reality through the light of God, and behave soberly and with self-control. They tremble with fear of God, full of anxiety and hope concerning their final goal, and pursue His pleasure by seeking to please Him and living in a way that shows their love for Him. In return, God loves them and causes other believers to love them. They are loved and esteemed by humanity and the jinn, and receive a warm welcome wherever they happen to be.

Prophet Joseph (Yusuf), upon him be peace, the truthful hero of *Sura Yusuf*, is mentioned five times in this *sura* as a man of perfect goodness and deep devotion. All of creation, including the Creator and the created, friend and foe, Earth and the heavens, testified to his strict self-control and self-supervision: *When Joseph reached his full manhood, We bestowed on him wisdom and knowledge. Thus do We reward those who are perfectly good [worshipping and acting in consciousness of being always seen by God]* (12:22). Here, the Almighty states that Prophet Joseph was a man of perfect goodness and self-control at the age of puberty. During his imprisonment in Egypt, every prisoner, whether good or evil, discerned the depth of his mind and purity of his spirit, and appealed to him to solve their problems: *Tell us the interpretation of events, including dreams, for we see you [to be] among those who are perfectly good* (12:36). Joseph succeeded in every trial he faced, and won a place in everyone's heart, both friend and foe.

Once more God mentions him as a man of perfect goodness, a perfect embodiment of goodness, as his character did not change when appointed to a high government post: *Thus We established Joseph in the land, to take possession of it where he pleased. We reach with Our mercy whom We will, and We never cause to be lost the reward of those who are perfectly good [worshipping and acting in consciousness of being always seen by God]* (12:56). When his brothers, who had always envied him, acknowledged his goodness and truthfulness even before they discovered that the charitable minister in the royal palace of Egypt was Joseph. They said: *O exalted sir. He has a father, aged and venerable; so take one of us instead of him, for we see that you are among those who are perfectly good* (12:78).

Lastly, as a man perfectly matured and having acquired full spiritual contentment, Prophet Joseph himself testified to God's blessings on him: *God has been indeed gracious to us. Whoever acts in fear of God and full submission to Him and is patient, surely God does not waste the reward of those who are perfectly good* (12:90).

It is inconceivable that an individual with such a sound heart could deviate or be deprived of God's blessing. Such a heart has the same meaning with respect to its owner as God's Supreme Throne has with respect to the universe, and is a polished mirror in which the Almighty looks in full appreciation. Such a mirror is not something to be discarded or allowed to break, for it is the essence and spirit of human reality and is praised by God.

In the following couplets, Rumi recalls this:

> The Truth says: I consider the heart,
> Not the form made from water and clay.
> You say: I have a heart within me, whereas
> The heart is above God's Throne, not below.

Huzn (Sadness or Sorrow)

Sufis use the word *huzn* (sadness) as the opposite of rejoicing and joy, and to express the pain one suffers while fulfilling his or her duties and realizing his or her ideals. Every perfected believer will continue to suffer this pain according to their degree of belief, and weave the tissue of life with the "threads" of sadness on the "loom" of time. In short, one will feel sadness until the spirit of the Muhammadan Truth has been breathed in all corners of the world, until the sighs of Muslims and other oppressed peoples cease, and the Divine rules are practiced in the daily lives of people.

This sadness will continue until the journey through the intermediate world of the grave (*'Alem al-Barzakh*) is completed, safe and sound, and the believer flies to the abode of eternal happiness and blessing without being detained by the Supreme Tribunal in the Hereafter. A believer's sorrows will never stop until the meaning of: *Praise be to God, Who has put grief away from us. Surely our Lord is All-Forgiving, Bountiful* (35:34) becomes manifest.

Sorrow or sadness arises from an individual's perception of what it means to be human, and grows in proportion to the degree of insight and discernment possessed by one who is conscious of his or her humanity. It is a necessary, significant dynamic that causes a believer to turn constantly to the Almighty and, perceiving the realities that cause sadness, seek refuge in Him and appeal to Him for help whenever he or she is helpless.

A believer aspires to very precious and valuable things, such as God's pleasure and eternal happiness, and therefore seeks to do a "very profitable business" with limited means in a short span of time (his or her life). The sorrows a believer experiences due to illness and pain, as well as various afflictions and misfortunes, resemble an effective medicine that wipes away one's sins and enables the eternalization of what is temporary, as well as the expansion of one's "drop-like" merit into an ocean. It can be said that a believer whose life has been spent in continuous sadness resembles, to a certain degree, the Prophets, for they also spent their lives in this state. How meaningful it is that the glory of mankind, upon him be peace and blessings, who spent his life in sorrow, is rightly described as "the Prophet of Sorrow" by Necib Fazil, the famous Turkish poet and writer.

Sadness protects a believer's heart and feelings from rust and decay, and compels him or her to concentrate on the inner world and on how to make progress along the way. It helps the traveler on the path of perfection to attain the rank of a pure spiritual life that another traveler cannot attain even after several forty-day periods of repentance and austerity. The Almighty considers the heart, not outward appearance or form. Among people's hearts, He considers the sad and broken ones and honors their owners with His presence, as stated in a narration: *I am near those with broken hearts.*[27]

Sufyan ibn Uyayna says: *God sometimes has mercy on a whole nation because of the weeping of a sad, broken-hearted one.*[28] This is so because sorrow arises in a sincere heart, and among the acts making one near to God, sadness or sorrow is the least vulnerable to being clouded by ostentation or one's desire to be praised. Part of every bounty and blessing of God is assigned to those who need it to purify that bounty or blessing of certain impurities. That part is called *zakat*, which literally means "to cleanse" or "to increase," for it cleanses one's belongings of those impurities that entered them while they were being earned or used, and causes them to increase as a blessing of God. Sadness or sorrow fulfills a similar role, for it is like the

---

[27] Al-'Ajluni, *Kashf al-Khafa'*, 1:203.

[28] Al-Qushayri, *Al-Risala,* 139.

part in one's mind or conscience that purifies and then maintains this purity and cleanliness.

It is narrated in the Torah that when God loves His servant, He fills his or her heart with the feeling of weeping; if He dislikes and gets angry with another, He fills his or her heart with a desire for amusement and play. Bishr al-Khafi says: *Sadness or sorrow is like a ruler. When it settles in a place, it does not allow others to reside there.*[29] A country with no ruler is in a state of confusion and disorder; a heart feeling no sorrow is ruined.

Was the one with the most sound and prosperous heart, upon him be peace and blessings, not always mournful and deep in thought? Prophet Jacob, upon him be peace, "climbed and went beyond the mountains" between him and his beloved son, Prophet Joseph, upon him be peace, on the wings of sorrow and witnessed the realization of a pleasing dream. The sighs of a sorrowful heart are regarded as having the same value and merit as the habitual recitations and remembrance of those who regularly and frequently worship God and the devotion and piety of ascetics who abstain from sin.

The truthful and confirmed one, upon him be peace and blessings, says that grief arising from worldly misfortune causes sins to be forgiven.[30] Based on this statement, one can see how valuable and meritorious are the sorrows that arise from one's sins, from the fear and love of God, and that pertain to the Hereafter. Some feel sorrow because they do not perform their duties of worship as perfectly as they should. They are ordinary believers. Others, who are among the distinguished, are sad because they are drawn toward that which is other than God. Still others feel sad because, while they feel themselves to be always in God's presence and never forget Him, they also are spending time among people in order to guide them to the Truth. They tremble with fear that they may upset the

---

[29] Ibid., 138.

[30] Nur al-Din Abu al-Hasan al-Haythami, *Majma' al-Zawa'id wa Manba' al Fawa'id,* 9 vols. (Beirut, 1967), 4:63.

balance between always being with God and being in the company of people. These are the purified ones who are responsible for guiding the people.

The first Prophet, Adam, upon him be peace, was the father of humanity and Prophets, and also the father of sorrow. He began his worldly life with sorrow: the fall from Paradise, Paradise lost, separation from God, and, thereafter, the heavy responsibility of Prophethood. He sighed with sorrow throughout his life. Prophet Noah, upon him be peace, found himself enveloped by sorrow when he became a Prophet. The waves of sorrow coming from the absolute unbelief of his people and their impending chastisement by God appeared in his chest as the waves of oceans. A day came, and those waves caused oceans to swell so high that they covered mountains and caused the earth to sink in grief. Prophet Noah became the Prophet of the Flood.

Prophet Abraham, upon him be peace, was as though programmed according to sorrow: sorrow arising from his struggle with Nimrod, being thrown into the fire and living always surrounded by "fires," leaving his wife and son in a desolate valley, being ordered to sacrifice his son, and many other sacred sorrows pertaining to the inner dimensions of reality and meanings of events. All of the other Prophets, such as Moses, David, Solomon, Zachariah, John the Baptist, and Jesus, upon them be peace, experienced life as a series or assemblage of sorrows, and lived it enveloped with sorrow. The Greatest of the Prophets and his followers tasted the greatest sorrows.

Khawf and *Khashya* (Fear and Reverence)

In Sufism, *khawf* (fear) denotes abstaining not only from all that is forbidden, but also from deeds from which it is advisable to refrain. It also signifies, as the opposite of hope or expectation, that a traveler on the path to Truth does not feel secure against deviation and thereby fears incurring Divine punishment in the Hereafter. As a result, the traveler refrains from conceit and self-praise.

According to Al-Qushayri, fear forces a traveler on the spiritual path to hold back and refrain from displeasing God. As such, fear pertains to the future. Fear arises from one's apprehension of being subjected to something displeasing, or uneasiness over not obtaining what is desired. In this sense also, fear pertains to the future. In many verses, the Qur'an points out the future results of one's deeds and actions, and thereby seeks to establish a world that embraces the future, one in which it is possible to discern the future with both its good and bad elements.

Implanting fear in the hearts of its followers, fear concerning their end or whether they will die as believing Muslims, the Qur'an warns them to be steadfast in their belief and practice of Islam. Many verses cause hearts to tremble with fear, and are like threads with which to knit the lace of life. For example: *Something will appear before them which they had never anticipated* (39:47); and *Say: Shall We tell you who will be the greatest losers by their works? Those whose efforts have been wasted in the life of the world while they thought they were doing good* (18:103-4). How happy and prosperous are those who knit the "laces" of their lives with these "threads"! With such warnings, the Qur'an orients us toward the Hereafter and encourages us to consider it more important than anything else.

In His luminous Speech, God Almighty uses fear as a whip to force us to His Presence and honor us with His company.[31] Like a mother's reproofs to her child that draws him or her to her warm, affectionate arms, this whip attracts the believer toward the depths of Divine Mercy and enriches him or her with the blessings and bounties of God; blessings and bounties that He compels humanity to deserve and receive out of His Mercy and Graciousness. For this reason, while every decree and command mentioned in the Qur'an and forced upon humanity originates in Divine Mercy and uplifts souls, they are also alarming and threatening.

One whose heart is full of fear and awe for the Almighty cannot be afraid of others, and is therefore freed from all useless and suffocating fear. In His luminous, hope-giving Speech, the Almighty tells people not to fear anything or anyone other than Him: *Have no fear of them. Fear Me, if you are true believers* (3:175); exhorts them not to suffer groundless phobias: *Fear Me alone* (2:40) and: *They fear their Lord, overseeing them from high, and they do all that they are commanded* (16:50); and praises those hearts that fear and hold only Him in awe: *They forsake their beds to cry unto their Lord in fear and hope* (32:16).

He praises such believers because those who arrange their lives according to their fear of God use their willpower carefully and strive to avoid sins. Such sensitive and careful souls fly in

---

[31] Fear is an essential ingredient in the stages of one's relationship with God. When the person is able to remain between and balance fear with hope, true education and training in the way of God begin. While it may seem to us that we are being "forced" by God into His Presence, in reality we are not, for this is only one of God's ways of reminding us of our true purpose. This is explained in the following *hadith*: *My relation to you is like a man who forces back those who are throwing themselves into a fire. You are throwing yourselves into a fire (by committing sins), but I am pulling you back.* This metaphor informs us that there are those who, although good-natured, believing, and inclined to good, cannot completely refrain from committing sins. To help them in their struggle to avoid sins, God, in His Mercy, may cause some misfortune to come upon them.

the heavens of God's approval and pleasure. The following is an appropriate saying by N. 'Abd al-Rahman ibn 'Ahmad al-Jami, the author of *Lujja*:

> If you are fearful of God's wrath, be steadfast in religion,
> For a tree holds fast to earth with its roots against violent storms.

The lowest degree of fear is that required by belief: *Fear Me, if you are (true) believers* (3:175). A somewhat higher degree of fear is that arising from knowledge or learning: *Among His servants the learned alone fear God truly* (35:28). The highest degree of fear is that combined with awe and arising from one's knowledge of God: *God orders you to fear Him in awe* (3:28).

Some Sufis divide fear into two categories: awe and reverence. Although these terms are very close in meaning, awe connotes the feeling that leads an initiate to flee toward God, while reverence causes an initiate to take refuge in Him. An initiate who continuously feels awe thinks of fleeing, while one seeking shelter strives to take refuge in Him. Those choosing to flee make progress on the path difficult for themselves, for they live an ascetic life and suffer the pains of separation from the Almighty. However, those holding Him in reverence drink the sweet, enlivening water of nearness, which comes from taking refuge in Him.

Perfect reverence was a characteristic of all Prophets. When in this state, the Prophets fell down nearly dead, as if they had heard the Trumpet of Israfil and had been brought before the full Majesty and Grandeur of the Truth. They were always conscious of the meaning of: *When His Lord revealed (His) glory to the mountain He sent it crashing down, and Moses fell down in a swoon* (7:143). Among those brought near to God, the one nearest to Him and the master of reverence, upon him be peace and blessings, said:

> I see what you do not see and hear what you do not hear. If only you knew with what the heavens creak and groan. In fact, they must do so, for there is not even the space of four fingers' breadth in the heavens where angels do not prostrate themselves. I swear by God that if you knew what I know (with respect to God's Grandeur), you

would laugh little but weep much. You would avoid lying with your
wives and cry out prayers unto God in fields and mountains.[32]

Here, the Prophet reveals his reverence that leads him to
take refuge in God, and describes the awe of others that causes
them to flee. Abu Dharr expresses this attitude of fleeing in his
addition to this Prophetic Tradition: *I wish I had been a tree
pulled out by the roots and cut into pieces.*

One whose soul is full of reverence and awe of God does
not commit sins, even if he does not seem to feel fear. Suhayb
was one of those overcome with awe of God. God's Messenger,
upon him be peace and blessings, praised him, saying: *What an
excellent servant Suhayb is! Even if he did not fear God, he
would not commit sins.*[33]

One who fears God sometimes sighs and sometimes weeps,
especially when alone, in an attempt to extinguish the pain of
being separated from Him, as well as the fire of Hell for him or
her, which is the greatest distance between him or her and God.
As stated in the Tradition: *A man who weeps for fear of God will
not enter Hell until the milk drawn (from a mammal) is put back
into the breasts (from which it was drawn).*[34] Shedding tears is
the most effective way of putting out the fires of Hell. A believer
sometimes confuses what he or she has done with what he or she
has not done and, fearing that the action has arisen from his or
her fancy or carnal self due to a personal failure to resist
temptation, feels great regret and seeks refuge in God. The
description of such souls is found in the following Tradition:

> When the verse: *Those who give what they give while their hearts
> are in awe, because they are to return to their Lord* (23:60) was
> revealed, 'A'isha, the Prophet's wife, asked the Prophet, upon him be
> peace and blessings: *Are those (who are in awe because they are to
> return to their Lord) those who commit such major sins as
> fornication, theft, and drinking alcohol?* The Prophet, the Glory of
> Mankind, answered: *No, 'A'isha. Those mentioned in the verse are*

---

[32] Tirmidhi, "Zuhd," 9; Ibn Maja, "Zuhd," 19.

[33] Al-'Ajluni, *Kashf al-Khafa'*, 323.

[34] Al-Tirmidhi, "Fada'il al-Jihad," 8; Al-Nasa'i, "Jihad," 8.

those who, although they perform the prescribed prayers, fast, and give alms, tremble with fear that such acts of worship may not be accepted by God.[35]

Abu Sulayman Darani says that although a servant must always be fearful (that God may not be pleased and therefore punish him or her) and hopeful (that God may be pleased), it is safer for one's heart to beat with fear and reverence.[36] Sharing the view of Darani, Shaykh Ghalib expresses his feelings of fear: *Open the eyes of my soul with a thousand-fold fear!*

---

[35] Al-Tirmidhi, "Tafsir al-Qur'an," 24.

[36] Al-Qushayri, *Al-Risala*, 128.

Raja (Hope or Expectation)

For a Sufi, *Raja* means waiting for that which he or she wholeheartedly desires to come into existence, acceptance of good deeds, and forgiveness of sins. Hope or expectation, both based on the fact that the individual is solely responsible for his or her errors and sins and that all good originates from and is of God's Mercy, is seen in this way: To avoid being caught in vices and faults and brought down by self-conceit over good deeds and virtues, an initiate must advance toward God through the constant seeking of forgiveness, prayer, avoidance of evil, and pious acts.

One's life must be lived in constant awareness of God's supervision, and one must knock tirelessly on His door with supplication and contrition. If an initiate successfully establishes such a balance between fear and hope, he or she will neither despair (of being a perfect, beloved servant of God) nor become conceited about any personal virtues and thereby neglect his or her responsibilities.

True expectation, possessed by those who are sincerely loyal to the Almighty, means seeking God's favor by avoiding sins. Such people undertake as many good deeds as possible, and then turn to God in expectation of His mercy. Others, however, have a false expectation. They spend their lives in sin, all the while expecting God's favor and reward, even though they perform none of the obligatory duties. They seem to believe that God is obligated to admit everyone to Paradise. Not only is this a false expectation, it is a mark of disrespect for the All-Merciful, the All-Compassionate, for such an expectation reflects their (misplaced) hope that God would violate His very nature to protect them from the consequences of their sins. To think that one is guaranteed a place in Paradise is a sin; to hope and strive for the same is commendable.

For Sufis, hope or expectation is not the same as a wish. A wish is a desire that may or may not be fulfilled, whereas hope or expectation is an initiate's active quest, through all lawful means, for the desired destination. In order that God, in His Mercy, will help him or her, the initiate does everything possible, with an almost Prophetic insight and consciousness, to cause all the doors of the Divine shelter to swing open. In other words, hope is the belief that, like His Attributes of Knowledge, Will, and Power, God's Mercy also encompasses all creation, and the expectation that he or she may be included in His special mercy: *My Mercy embraces all things* (7:156); and in a *hadith qudsi*, a Prophetic saying whose meaning was directly revealed by God, which reads: *God's Mercy exceeds His Wrath.*[37] Indifference to such Mercy, from which even devils hope to benefit in the Hereafter, and despairing of being enveloped by it, which amounts to denying it, is an unforgivable sin.

Hope means that an initiate seeks the ways to reach the Almighty in utmost reliance on His being the All-Munificent and the All-Loving. M. Lutfi Efendi expresses his hope as follows:

> Be kind to me, O my Sovereign,
> do not cease favoring the needy and destitute!
> Does it befit the All-Kind and Munificent to stop favoring His slaves?

Those who are honored by such Divine kindness can be considered as having found a limitless treasure—especially at a time when a person has lost whatever he or she has, is exposed to misfortune, or feels in his or her conscience the pain of being unable to do anything good or to be saved from evil. In short, when there are no means left that can be resorted to, and all of the ways out end in the Producer of all causes and means, hope illuminates the way, like a heavenly mount that carries one to peaks normally impossible to reach.

Here I cannot help but recall the hope expressed in the last words of Imam Shafi'i in Gaza:

---

[37] Al-Bukhari, "Tawhid," 55; Muslim, "Tawba," 14-16, Ibn Maja, "Zuhd," 35.

> When my heart was hardened and my ways were blocked,
> I made my hope a ladder to Your forgiveness;
> My sins are too great in my sight, but
> When I weigh them against Your forgiveness,
> Your forgiveness is much greater than my sins.[38]

It is advisable for one to feel fear in order to abandon sin and turn to God. One should cherish hope when falling into the pit of despair and the signs of death appear. Fear removes any feeling of security against God's punishment, and hope saves the believer from being overwhelmed by despair. For this reason, one may be fearful even when all obligatory duties have been performed perfectly; one may be hopeful although he or she has been less than successful in doing good deeds. This is what is stated in the following supplication of Yahya ibn Mu'adh:

> O God! The hope I feel in my heart when I indulge in sin is usually greater than the hope I feel after performing the most perfect deeds. This is because I am "impaired" with flaws and imperfections, and never sinless and infallible. When I am stained with sin, I rely on no deeds or actions but Your forgiveness. How should I not rely on Your forgiveness, seeing that You are the Generous One?[39]

According to many, hope is synonymous with cherishing a good opinion of the Divine Being.[40] This is related in the following *hadith qudsi*: *I treat My servant in the way he thinks of Me treating him.*[41] A man once dreamed that Abu Sahl was enjoying indescribable bounties and blessings, and asked him how he had attained such a degree of reward. Abu Sahl answered: *By means of my good opinion of my Lord.*[42] That is why we can say that if hope is a means for God's manifestation of His infinitely profound Mercy, a believer should never relinquish it. Even if

---

[38] Muhammad ibn Ahmad ibn 'Uthman al-Dhahabi, *Siyar 'Alam al-Nubala'*, 25 vols. (Beirut, 1992), 1:150.

[39] Al-Qushayri, *Al-Risala*, 133.

[40] In other words, one should regard Him as an All-Merciful and All-Forgiving Lord, rather than as an All-Punishing One.

[41] Al-Bukhari, "Tawhid", 15; Muslim, "Tawba," 1; Al-Tirmidhi, "Dawa'at," 132.

[42] Al-Qushayri, *Al-Risala*, 134.

one always performs good deeds and preserves his or her sincerity and altruism, since these are the accomplishments of a finite being with limited capacities, they have little importance when compared with God's forgiveness.

Fear and hope are two of the greatest gifts of God that He may implant in a believer's heart. If there is a gift greater than these, it is that one should preserve the balance between fear and hope and then use them as two wings of light with which to reach God.

Zuhd (Asceticism)

Zuhd, which literally means renouncing worldly pleasures and resisting carnal desires, is defined by Sufis as indifference to worldly appetites, living an austere life, choosing to refrain from sin in fear of God, and despising the world's carnal and material aspects. Asceticism is also described as renouncing this world's temporary ease and comfort for the sake of eternal happiness in the Hereafter. The first step in asceticism is the intention to avoid what has been forbidden and to engage only in what has been allowed. The second and final step is to be circumspect, extremely careful even when engaging in what is allowed.

An ascetic is steadfast in fulfilling his or her responsibilities, is not defeated by misfortune, and avoids the traps of sin and evil encountered during the journey. With the exception of unbelief and misguidance, an ascetic is pleased with how the Creator decides to treat him or her, seeks to attain God's pleasure and the eternal abode through the blessings and bounties that He bestows, and directs others to the absolute Truth. In the ear of his or her heart, the Divine announcement is echoed: *Say: The enjoyment of this world is short; and the Hereafter is better for him who obeys God's commandments in fear of Him* (4:77). The command: *Seek the abode of the Hereafter in that which God has given you, and forget not your portion of the world* (28:77) radiates itself through all the cells of his or her brain. The Divine warning: *This life of the world is but a pastime and a game, but the home of the Hereafter, that is Life if they but knew* (29:64) penetrates his or her innermost senses.

Some have described asceticism as observing the rules of Shari'a, even in moments of depression and especially during financial difficulties, and living for others or considering their well-being and happiness while enjoying well-being and comfort. Others have defined it as thankfulness for God's bounties and fulfilling the accompanying obligations, and refraining from hoarding money and goods (except for the intention to serve, exalt, and promote Islam).

Such renowned Sufi leaders as Sufyan al-Thawri regarded asceticism as the action of a heart dedicated to God's approval and pleasure and closed to worldly ambitions, rather than as being content with simple food and clothes.[43] According to these Sufis, there are three signs of a true ascetic: feeling no joy at worldly things acquired or grief over worldly things missed, feeling no pleasure when praised or displeasure when criticized or blamed, and preferring to serve God over everything else.

Like fear and hope, asceticism is an action of the heart; however, asceticism differs in that it affects one's acts and is displayed through them. Whether consciously or unconsciously, a true ascetic tries to follow the rules of asceticism in all acts, such as eating and drinking, going to bed and getting up, talking and keeping silent, and remaining in retreat or with people. An ascetic shows no inclination toward worldly attractions. Rumi expresses this in the following apt words:

> What is the world? It is heedlessness of God;
> Not clothes, nor silver coin, nor children, nor women.
> If you have worldly possessions in the name of God,
> Then the Messenger said: *How fine is the property a righteous man has!*[44]
> The water in a ship causes it to sink,
> While the water under it causes it to float.

Possessing worldly means or wealth is not contrary to asceticism—if the owner can control his or her possessions and is not over powered by them. Nevertheless, the glory of humanity, upon him be peace and blessings, the truest ascetic in all respects, chose to live as the

---

[43] Ibid., 115.

[44] Ibn Hanbal, *Musnad*, 4:197.

poorest of his people, for he had to set the most excellent example for his community—especially for those charged with
spreading the truth. Thus, he would not lead others to think that
the sacred mission of Prophethood could be abused to earn
worldly advantage.

He also had to follow his predecessors, who proclaimed: *My
reward is only due from God* (10:72; 11:29), and to set an
example for those future scholars who would convey his Message. For these and similar other reasons, he led an austere life.
How beautiful are the following couplets by Busayri, which
express how the Prophet preserved his innocence and indifference, even at the time of absolute need and poverty:

> Not to feel hunger, he wound a girdle around his belly
> Over the stones pressing upon his blessed stomach.
> Huge mountains wishing themselves gold offered themselves to him,
> But he—that noble man—remained indifferent to them.
> His urgent needs decisively showed his asceticism,
> For those needs were not able to impair his innocence.
> How could needs have been able to invite to the world the one
> But for whom the world would not have come into being out of non-existence?

There are many beautiful sayings on asceticism. The following, with which we conclude this topic, belongs to 'Ali, the
fourth Caliph and cousin of the Prophet, upon him be peace and
blessings:

> The soul weeps in desire of the world despite the fact that
> It knows salvation lies in renouncing it and what is in it.
> A man will have no abode to dwell in after his death
> Except that which he builds before he dies.
> Our goods—we hoard them to bequeath to heirs;
> Our houses—we build them to be ruined by time.
> There are many towns built and then ruined;
> Their builders—death has come upon them.
> Every soul—even if it somehow fears death,
> It cherishes ambitions to strengthen its desire to live.
> Man exhibits his ambitions but time obliterates them;
> Man's soul multiplies them but death puts an end to them.

*O God! Show us the truth as being true and enable us to follow it.
Show us falsehood as being false, and provide us with the means to
refrain from it. Amen, O Most Compassionate of the Compassionate.*

Taqwa (Piety)

Taqwa is derived from *wiqaya*, which means self-defense and avoidance. Sufis define it as protecting oneself from God's punishment by performing His commands and observing His prohibitions. Besides its literal and technical meanings, in religious books we find the meanings of piety and fear used interchangeably. In fact, *taqwa* is a comprehensive term denoting a believer's strict observance of the commandments of the Shari'a and the Divine laws of nature and life. Such a person seeks refuge in God against His punishment, refrains from acts leading to Hellfire, and performs acts leading to Paradise. Again, the believer purifies all outer and inner senses so that none of them can associate partners with God, and avoids imitating the worldviews and lifestyles of unbelievers. In its comprehensive meaning, *taqwa* is the only and greatest standard of one's nobility and worth: *The noblest, most honorable of you in the sight of God is the most advanced of you in taqwa* (49:13).

The concept of—even the actual word—*taqwa* is unique to the Qur'an and the religious system of Islam. Its comprehensive meaning encompasses the spiritual and material; its roots are established in this world, while its branches, leaves, flowers, and fruit are located in the Hereafter. One cannot understand the Qur'an without considering the meaning or content of the fascinating and wonderful concept of *taqwa*, and one cannot be *muttaqi* (pious) if one does not adhere consciously and continually to the practices and concepts outlined in the Qur'an.

In its very beginning, the Qur'an opens its door to the pious: *This is the Book about and in which there is no doubt, a guidance for the pious* (2:2), and calls on people to live in accordance with it so that they may be pious: *O men! Worship your Lord, Who created you and those before you, so that you may be pious (and protect yourselves from His punishment)* (2:21).

The most lovable act in God's sight is piety (*taqwa*), His most purified servants are the pious, and His peerless message to them is the Qur'an. In this world, the pious have the Qur'an; in the Hereafter, they enjoy God's vision and pleasure. The pleasure felt in the conscience and spirit is another gift of piety, and in order to recall the importance of piety, the Almighty decrees: *Fear God and be devoted to Him as He should be feared and devoted to* (3:101).

Piety, which is the conscious performance of good and the avoidance of evil, prevents individuals from joining the lowest of the low and causes them to advance on the path of the highest of the high. For this reason, one who attains piety has found the source of all good and blessing. The following is another testimony to this fact:

> To whomever God has given religion and piety,
> He has realized his aims in this world and the next.
> Whoever is a soldier of God and pious,
> He is prosperous and truly guided, not wretched.
> Whoever has nothing to do with piety,
> His existence is but a shame and disgrace.
> One lifeless with respect to truth is not truly alive;
> Only one who has found a way to God is alive.

Piety is an invaluable treasure, the matchless jewel in a priceless treasure of precious stones, a mysterious key to all doors of virtue, and a mount on the way to Paradise. Its value is so high that, among other life-giving expressions, the Qur'an mentions it 150 times, each time resembling a ray of light penetrating our minds and spirits.

In its limited sense, *taqwa* means sensitivity to the commandments of the Shari'a and refraining from acts that deprive one of Divine reward and result in God's punishment. The verse: *Those who refrain from major sins and shameful deeds* (42:37) expresses one aspect of this basic religious virtue; the verse: *Those who believe and do good deeds* (10:9) points to the other.

Strict observance of obligatory religious duties and refraining from major sins are the two necessary and complementary foundations of *taqwa*. As for minor sins, which the Qur'an calls *lamam* (small offenses), there are many Prophetic declarations, such as: *A servant cannot be truly pious unless he refrains from certain permissible things lest he should commit risky things*,[45] that warn people to be careful.

Perfect sincerity or purity of intention can be attained by avoiding any association of partners with God, while perfect piety can be achieved by refraining from all doubtful and risky deeds. According to the Prophetic saying: *The lawful is evident and the forbidden is also evident. Between these two are things which most of the people do not know whether they are lawful or forbidden*, a truly righteous, spiritual life depends on being sensitive to matters about which there is some doubt. The Tradition above points out that the Legislator of the Shari'a has clearly explained in broad terms what is allowed and what is forbidden. However, as many things are not clearly allowed or forbidden, only those who avoid doubtful things can live a truly religious life. Using a simile in the continuation of the Tradition, the prince of the two worlds, upon him be peace and blessings, said:

> It is possible for one who does doubtful things to commit forbidden acts, just as it is possible for the flock of a shepherd pasturing near a field belonging to another or the public to enter that field. Know that each king has a private area under his protection; the private area of God is forbidden things. Also know that there is a part of flesh in the body. If it is healthy, the body will become healthy; if it is ailing, the body will be ailing. That part is the heart.[46]

In light of this basic foundation for a healthy spiritual life, perfect piety can be obtained by avoiding doubtful things and minor sins. In order to do this, however, one must know what is lawful and what is forbidden, and have a certain knowledge of

---

[45] Al-Tirmidhi, "Qiyama," 19; Ibn Maja, "Zuhd," 24.

[46] Al-Bukhari, "Iman," 39; Muslim, "Musaqat," 107, 108.

God. We can find the combination of piety and knowledge in these two verses: *The noblest, most honorable of you in the sight of God is the most advanced of you in taqwa* (49:13), and: *Only the learned among His servants fear and revere God* (35:28). Piety brings honor and nobility, and knowledge leads one to fear and revere God. Individuals who combine piety and knowledge in their hearts are mentioned in the Qur'an as those who pass the test of piety: *They are those whose hearts God has tested for piety* (49:3).

In the context of worship and obedience, piety means purity of heart, spiritual profundity, and sincerity. In the context of refraining from what is unlawful, piety means being determined not to commit sins and to avoid doubtful things. For this reason, each of the following may be considered an aspect of piety: A servant must

- Seek only God's approval and pleasure, and not set his or her heart upon whatever is other than Him.

- Observe all commandments of the Shari'a.

- Do whatever is necessary to achieve the objective, and be convinced that only God will create the result. Thus one cannot be a fatalist (i.e., one cannot neglect to perform whatever is necessary to obtain a certain result, and must take all necessary measures against possible misfortune or defeat) or a pure rationalist and positivist (Mu'tazili) who attributes all human acts and accomplishments to oneself by denying God any part in them.

- Be alert to whatever may divert him or her from God.

- Be alert to the carnal pleasures that may lead to the realm of the forbidden.

- Ascribe all material and spiritual accomplishments to God.

- Not consider himself or herself as superior to anyone else.

- Not pursue anything other than God and His pleasure.

· Follow the guide of all, upon him be peace and blessings, without condition or reservation.

· Renew himself or herself, and continuously control his or her spiritual life by studying and reflecting on God's acts and works as well as on His laws of nature and life.

· Remember death, and live with the conscious knowledge that it may happen at any time.

In conclusion, *taqwa* is the heavenly water of life, and a *muttaqi* (pious one) is the fortunate one who has found it. Only a few individuals have achieved the blessing of this attainment. A poet said:

> God Almighty says: The great among you are those who are pious.
> The last abode of the pious will be Paradise and their drink *kawthar*.

> *O God! Include us among Your pious servants who were sincere in all their religious acts.*

Wara' (Abstinence)

Wara' is defined as holding oneself back from unbecoming, unnecessary things[47], as strictly refraining from what is unlawful and forbidden, or abstaining from all doubtful things lest one should commit a forbidden act. The Islamic principle: *Abandon what you doubt and prefer what you have no doubt about*,[48] and the Prophetic saying: *What is lawful is evident and what is forbidden is also evident*, explain the basis of *wara'*.[49]

Some Sufis define *wara'* as the conviction of the truth of Islamic tenets, being straightforward in one's beliefs and acts, being steadfast in observing Islamic commandments, and being circumspect in one's relations with God Almighty. Others define it as not being heedless of God even for one twinkling of the eye, and others as permanently closing themselves to all that is not Him, as not abasing oneself before anyone except Him (for the fulfillment of one's needs or other reasons), and as advancing until reaching God without getting mired down by one's ego, carnal self and desires, or the world.

> Always refrain from begging from people,
> Beg only from your Lord Who is the All-Munificent.
> Renounce the pomp and luxuries of the world
> Which will certainly go as they have come.

We can also interpret *wara'* as basing one's life on engaging in what is necessary and useful, as acting in consciousness of the real nature of useless, fleeting, and transient things. This is

---

[47] It is very difficult to define this rather ambiguous phrase, as such "things" must be defined within the context of the time in which one lives and within the conditions with which one is faced.

[48] Al-Bukhari, "Buyu'," 3; Al-Tirmidhi, "Qiyama," 60.

[49] Al-Tirmidhi, "Zuhd," 11; Ibn Maja, "Fitan," 12.

stated in the Tradition: *The beauty of being a good Muslim is abandoning what is of no use to him.*

The writer of the *Pandname*, Farid al-Din al-Attar, explains this principle very beautifully:

> *Wara'* gives rise to fear of God,
> One without *wara'* is subject to humiliation.
> Whoever virtuously follows the way of *wara'*,
> Whatever he does is for the sake of God.
> One who desires love and friendship of God,
> Without *wara'*, he is false in his claim of love.

Wara' relates to both the inner and outer aspects of a believer's life and conduct. A traveler on the path of *wara'* must reach the peaks of *taqwa*; his or her life must reflect a strict observance of the Shari'a's commands and prohibitions; his or her actions must be for the sake of God; his or her heart and feelings must be purged of whatever is other than God; he or she must always feel the company of the "Hidden Treasure."

In other words, the traveler abandons those thoughts and conceptions that do not lead to Him, keeps aloof from those scenes that do not remind them of Him, does not listen to speeches that are not about Him, and is not occupied with that which does not please Him. Such a degree of *wara'* leads one directly and quickly to God Almighty, Who declared to Prophet Moses: *Those who desire to get near to Me have not been able to find a way better than wara' and zuhd (asceticism).*

The abstinence known by humanity during the Age of Happiness[50] was perfectly observed by the blessed generations following the Companions, and became an objective of almost every believer. It was during this period that Bishr al-Khafi's sister asked Ahmad ibn Hanbal:

> *O Imam, I usually spin (wool) on the roof of my house at night. At that time, some officials pass by with torches in their hands, and I happen to benefit, even unwillingly, from the light of their torches.*

---

[50] In Islamic literature, the Age of Happiness refers to the time when the Prophet lived and led his community.

Does this mean that I mix into my earnings something gained through a religiously unlawful way? The great Imam wept bitterly at this question and replied: *Something doubtful even to such a minute degree must not find a way into the house of Bishr al-Khafi.*[51]

It was also during this period that people shed tears for the rest of their lives because they had cast a single glance at something forbidden, and people who vomited a piece of unlawful food that they had swallowed in ignorance wept for days. As related by 'Abd Allah ibn Mubarak, a great traditionist and ascetic, a man traveled from Merv (Turkmenistan) to Makka in order to return to its owner an item that he had put in his pocket by mistake. There were many who gave life-long service to those to whom they thought they owed something, such as Fudayl ibn 'Iyad. Biographies of saints, such as *Hilyat al-Awliya'* (The Necklace of Saints) by Abu Nu'aym al-Isfahani, and *al-Tabaqat al-Kubra* (The Greatest Compendium) by Imam al-Sharani, are full of the accounts of such heroes of abstinence.

---

[51] Al-Qushayri, *Al-Risala*, 111.

'Ibada, *'Ubudiya*, and *'Ubuda* (Worship, Servanthood, and Deep Devotion)

Although some view worship, servanthood, and devotion as synonymous, most Sufi scholars and masters say that these words have different meanings and connotations. *'Ibada* (worship) means fulfilling God's commands in one's daily life and fulfilling the obligations of being His servant, while *'ubuda* (servanthood) is interpreted as living in the consciousness of being a servant. Thus, one who observes his or her religious duties is called *'abid* (worshipper), while one who lives in consciousness of being a servant of God is usually called *'abd* (servant).

There is another, more subtle difference between worship and servanthood. Acts of worship consist of all financial and physical duties: those requiring sufficient financial resources and physical ability, and that are accomplished with difficulty, in fear and hope, and with the intention of pleasing God (e.g., the five daily prayers, fasting, alms-giving, pilgrimage to Makka, offering a sacrifice, and mentioning or reciting God's Names). A servant of God, however, understands these responsibilities or acts of worship in a different manner: each fulfillment of such a duty has a deeper (inner) dimension that requires a certain degree of consciousness and awareness on the part of the servant.

The deepest dimension of religious duties and demands is devotion, which requires total care and awareness. Ibn al-Farid states: *The acts of worship and duties of servanthood required by every station or rank that I have reached during my spiritual journey have been fulfilled by my devotion.*

Some Sufis have defined worship as the servanthood of ordinary people, servanthood as the duty required by being a servant of God and carried out by individuals possessing insight

and awareness, and devotion as the responsibility of those distinguished by their nearness to God. The first group contains those
striving to advance on the path of God; the second group contains
those whose mental and spiritual attitudes allow them to
overcome all seemingly insurmountable obstacles and difficulties
they encounter; the third group contains those whose mental and
spiritual states cause them to turn to God wholeheartedly and
with a profound feeling of being in His company.

Other Sufis have summed up the above explanations in two
terms: worship of the Absolute Divine Essence, and worship of
the Restricted Divine Attributes. The first term means always
being conscious of the relationship between the Creator and
created, the Worshipped One and the worshipper, the Overseeing
and the overseen, the Sustaining and the sustained, and
thinking, feeling, and acting in the most profound awareness of
these relationships. The second term means fulfilling one's daily
duties as required by this awareness, which causes one's
awareness to increase. Those performing these duties can be
categorized by their intention, resolution, determination, and
sincerity as follows: those who desire to enter Paradise, those
who hope to be rescued from Hellfire, those who love and stand
in awe of God, and those who feel that they must do so as a
requirement of the relationship between God as the Creator
(Who alone deserves worship) and human beings (created
beings who must worship their Creator).

Each group has another name: merchants, slaves, lovers, and
the devoted or faithful. These words of Rabi'a al-'Adawiya, a
female Muslim saint who lived during the second century of
Islam, are quite appropriate:

> O Lord. I swear by the beauty of nearness to You that I have not
> worshipped You either for fear of Hell or out of the desire for
> Paradise. I have worshipped You because of You.

Servanthood is a source of honor and dignity for men and
women. Nothing is more esteemed or valuable than being
honored with servanthood and devotion to God. Although other,
more valuable ranks may be conferred for a limited time,

servanthood is constant and continuous, and therefore the most valuable rank. This is why God Almighty described the best of creation, upon him be peace and blessings, as His servant in the most beautiful words: *There is no deity but God, and Muhammad is His servant and Messenger*, and He crowned his servanthood and these blessed words with his Messengership.

Also, when inviting the Prophet, the glory of humanity and the peerless, unique one of time and creation, to honor the heavens by the Ascension,[52] He began His invitation with the complimentary phrase: *He carried His servant by night* (17:1), thereby referring to the matchless greatness of his servanthood. This is even more meaningful, as on this occasion when space and time were almost transcended and the all-pervasive light of Divine Grace and Beauty welcomed him, God Almighty again stressed his servanthood and declared: *He revealed to His servant what He revealed* (53:10).

Rumi does not present himself as a saint or an individual of profound spiritual depth, but as a servant:

> I have become a servant, become a servant, become a servant;
> I have bowed and doubled myself up with serving You.
> Servants or slaves rejoice when they are emancipated;
> Whereas I rejoice when I become Your servant.

According to some, the following should also be considered when discussing worship and servanthood. A servant should:

- Be aware of his or her faults and worry about them even if he or she thinks that the acts of worship have been performed perfectly.

- Endeavor to worship perfectly, and then attribute to God whatever is achieved in the name of servanthood. Each moment of life should be spent in the awareness of his or her being a servant to the eternal Lordship of God.

---

[52] The Ascension (*mi'raj*) was a miraculous event during which the Prophet journeyed throughout the realms of existence to God.

· Regard all facets of existence as shadows of the Light of His existence, and never attribute to oneself the existence of anything or any accomplishment. There should be no self-pride concerning the blessings conferred, or despair concerning the withholding of all spiritual gifts and radiances.

· Be aware of the honor and dignity of being attached to Him, and never imagine being honored with other kinds of ranks.

No other rank or honor is as great as or greater than servant-hood. If any rank or honor may be considered as such, it may be freedom, but only in the meaning of not setting one's heart on anything other than God and renouncing whatever is other than Him. Those who have not made great progress on the path to God can only feel freedom, while those who have reached the destination experience it fully. I think that the true freedom to which one must aspire, one that will be appropriate for his or her grade and dignity, is this one. A friend of God draws attention to this fact:

O son! Unchain yourself and become free!
How much longer will you remain a slave of silver and gold?

Junayd al-Baghdadi warns that unless one is freed from slavery to others, one cannot attain true servanthood to God.[53] Another friend of God expresses the meaning of servanthood and freedom by advising that a servant of God should never consider any other than God in all of his or her thoughts, imaginings, feelings, and manners:

If you would like to beat the drum of honor, go beyond the wheel of stars;
As this circle filled with rings is a drum of humiliation.

O God! Enable us to attain to what is loved by and pleasing to You.

---

[53] Al-Qushayri, Al-Risala, 201.

Muraqaba (Self-Supervision)

Muraqaba has been defined as watching, supervising, controlling, and living in the consciousness of being controlled (by God). Sufis take this further, defining it as setting one's heart solely on God, abandoning any attachment to that which is other than Him, denying to one's carnal self all that is forbidden, acting in the certainty that the Divine Knowledge encompasses all things, and living in accordance with Divine commandments.

We can also interpret *muraqaba* as trying to observe whatever God wills, and leading a life of unwavering sincerity in the consciousness of His constant supervision. Such an attitude is possible when the servant knows that the Almighty is aware of all that he or she does, says, knows, and thinks, as stated in the Qur'an: *In whatever state you may be, and whichever part of the Qur'an you recite, and whatever deed you do, We are witnesses over you when you are deeply engrossed therein* (10:61).

If *muraqaba* means closing one's heart to all that displeases Him and separates one from Him, and opening the spirit to receive the radiances, gifts, and favors coming from Him, then we must close what we must and open what we must. The first steps to *muraqaba* are to accept as great what God has decreed as great, to accept as worthless what He has decreed as worthless, and to prefer His Will and desires over our own. Thinking of the depth of God's Mercy increases and strengthens one's love of God and the desire to worship Him, and fear and be in awe of Him causes one to lose any appetite for sin and to live a careful life. *Muraqaba* leads men and women to discard anything that harms their worship, and to maintain the purity of their thoughts, actions, and intentions even when they are alone, in the consciousness of His continual observation.

Muraqaba is one of the most important and direct ways of reaching God without a guide. It resembles the type of sainthood attained through succession to the Prophetic mission, which is conveying the Divine Message to people, without following a spiritual order. Such travelers can turn to God at any time or place in awareness of their helplessness and destitution, and be admitted to a "private meeting" with Him based on their need. They feel God's constant supervision while they are watching nature, and so avoid whatever is other than Him; they are deaf to all sounds and voices that are unrelated to Him; and they praise His Beauty and Grace, and regard it as useless to mention something that is not concerned with Him.

As a matter of fact, if one's eyes do not remind one of His Seeing, one's ears of His Hearing, and one's tongue of His Speech, how can these organs be used other than as pieces of flesh? Rumi says:

> God Almighty described Himself as the All-Seeing in order to warn you against evil, He described Himself as the All-Hearing to admonish you not to say anything bad, and He described Himself as the All-Knowing to inform you that He knows you and therefore to exhort you to be alert to corrupt thoughts and considerations.

Rumi regards self-supervision as a protecting screen from evil emotions, thoughts, passions, and acts, and considers it the safest way to be attentive to Divine rights.

The first step in self-supervision is voluntary submission to the Divine Will in the conviction that He is present everywhere and is aware of all our thoughts, intentions, and deeds: *God is Watcher over all things* (33:52). The second step is to turn to God with a heart at rest and patiently anticipate the flow of Divine gifts and blessings into one's heart.

This does not require any physical or spiritual attachment to or relationship with a guide, or the regular recitation of God's Names. However, if one wishes to follow a guide and regularly recite His Names in accordance with the Shari'a, it will certainly be much better. To the extent that an initiate, whether on the first or second step, can act according to the meaning of the Prophetic Tradition, *Perfect goodness is that you worship as if seeing God, for even if you do not see Him, He certainly sees you,*[54] and that, always seeing himself or herself as helpless, destitute, and needy before God, believes Him to be the sole point of reliance and source of help, he or she will travel safely on the path of self-supervision and therefore be secure against deviation. Over time, those who follow such a path will acquire a peace of heart that will allow their conscience to remain open to Divine gifts and receive radiances from the One of Unity.

One of the most important mechanisms of self-supervision is *muhasaba* (self-criticism). As this method of self-control allows believers to become aware of personal faults and their causes, they can find the truth in their hearts and then display it in their conduct. In this spirit, the meaning and mystery of *Glory be to Him Who sees me, knows my place and hears my speech* manifests itself. Such people know that the Divine Knowledge and Will always keep them under control and, regardless of location or action, seek only God's pleasure by trying to act in accordance with His wishes.

---

[54] Al-Bukhari, "Iman," 37; Muslim, "Iman," 1.

Ikhlas (Sincerity or Purity of Intention)

Ikhlas has been interpreted as being upright, sincere, and pure; being distant from show and ostentation in one's intention and conduct; and being immune to whatever clouds or fouls the heart. Purity of intention, straightforwardness in thought, pursuit of no worldly gains in one's relationship with God, and loyalty in servanthood to God are also included in this.

Ikhlas requires that one seeks nothing worldly while worshipping and obeying God, that one fulfills the duty of servanthood only because God orders it, and that one remains silent concerning any personal experiences of God's special treatment and special gifts and seeks only His approval and pleasure.

Sincerity is one of the most significant qualities of those who are most faithful or loyal to God; loyalty is regarded as the source, and sincerity as the sweet water that originates from it. The most eloquent of humanity, upon him be peace and blessings, declared that one who drinks uninterruptedly from this water for forty days will find channels of wisdom opened from his or her heart to their tongue, and that such a person will always speak wisely.

Loyalty or faithfulness is the primary attribute of Prophethood, and sincerity is its most lustrous dimension. Sincerity is innate in the Prophets; all other people try to obtain it during their lifetime. Among them, for example, the Qur'an describes the Prophet Moses as *one made sincere* (19:51).

Faithfulness and sincerity were as intrinsic and essential to the Prophets as air and water are to the lives of those who communicate the Prophets' message to others in every age. In addition, they were the Prophets' most important sources of power.

The Prophets were convinced that they could not take one step forward without sincerity, and the representatives of the cause of Prophethood must believe that they will be able to achieve nothing without it. Faithfulness and sincerity are two wings, or two deep oceans extending from Divine Favor and Grace to an individual's heart. One who can sail on these oceans or fly with these wings will reach the destination, for they are under God's protection. God values that which is done to please Him, regardless of its apparent size or importance, He is concerned with the quality, not the quantity of the deeds. Therefore, He values a small deed done sincerely over many deeds done insincerely.

Sincerity is an attitude of the heart, and God views an individual according to the inclination of one's heart. The Prophet, upon him be peace and blessings, declares: *Assuredly, God does not consider your bodies, nor your appearances. Rather, He considers your hearts.*[55] Sincerity is a mysterious Divine credit granted to those who are pure-hearted in order to increase what is little and to deepen what is shallow, and to give finite (limited) worship infinite reward. One can use sincerity to purchase the most valuable things in the markets of this world and the next, for it is esteemed, welcomed, and respected where others suffer great misery. This mysterious power of sincerity caused God's Messenger, upon him be peace and blessings, to declare: *Be sincere in your religion; little work (with sincerity) is enough for you,*[56] and: *Be sincere in your deeds, for God only accepts what is done with sincerity.*[57]

If we consider a deed to be a body, sincerity is its soul. If a deed represents one wing of a pair of wings, sincerity is the other. A body without soul is of no worth, and nothing can fly with only one wing. How fine are Mawlana Jalal al-Din al-Rumi's words:

---

[55] Muslim, "Birr," 33; Ibn Maja, "Zuhd," 9.

[56] 'Abd al-Ra'uf Munawi, *Fayd al-Qadir*, 6 vols. (Beirut 1093 AH / 1682 CE) 1:216.

[57] Ibid., 1:217.

You should be sincere in all your deeds,
So that the Majestic Lord may accept them.
Sincerity is the wing of the bird of the acts of obedience.
Without a wing, how can you fly to the abode of prosperity?

The following words of Bayazid al-Bistami are also very apt:

I worshipped my Lord for thirty years with all my strength. Then I heard a voice saying: *O Bayazid! The treasures of God Almighty are full of acts of worship. If you intend to reach Him, see yourself as insignificant at the door of God and be sincere in your deeds.*

For some, sincerity involves hiding from others when performing supererogatory deeds and avoiding all show and ostentation. For others, it means that whether one is or is not being seen while performing religious deeds is not important. Still for others, it means being so involved in worship or religious deeds when seeking God's pleasure that one does not even remember whether one should be sincere or not.

Self-supervision is an essential dimension of sincerity, and a truly sincere person does not consider any possible spiritual pleasure that may arise, or speculate upon whether such acts will ensure entrance to Paradise. Sincerity is a mystery between God and a servant, and God puts it in the hearts of those He loves. One whose heart is awakened to sincerity does not worry about being praised or accused, exalted or debased, aware or unaware of deeds, or of being rewarded. Such a person does not change, and behaves in the same way in public and in private.

Istiqama (Straightforwardness)

People of truth have interpreted *istiqama* (straightforwardness) as avoiding all deviation and extremes, and as following in
the footsteps of the Prophets, the faithful, the witnesses (of
truth), and the righteous (in belief) in their religious deeds and
daily lives. The verse: *Those who declare: "Our Lord is God,"
and afterwards are candid, the angels descend upon them
(saying): "Fear not nor grieve, and good tidings to you of
Paradise which you were promised"* (41:30) informs us that
angels will receive in the Hereafter those who have acknowledged God's Lordship, affirmed His Unity, and followed the
Prophets in their beliefs, deeds, and daily lives. Such a blame-
less life will cause these people to receive the good
tidings of Paradise at a time when all people will tremble with
fear and worry on the Day of Judgment.

An individual's conduct becomes straightforward by
performing religious duties; one's ego (inner self)
becomes straightforward by following the truth of the
Shari'a; one's spirit becomes straightforward by acting in
accordance with knowing God; and one's innermost senses or
faculties becomes straightforward by complying with the spirit
of the Shari'a. The difficulty in being straightforward at all of
these levels caused the Prophet, the most straightforward
of people, upon him be peace and blessings, to say: *Sura
Hud and others similar to it have made me old,*[58] thereby
referring to the Divine command: *Be straightforward as you are
commanded*, which is found in *sura Hud* (11:112).

The Prophet, upon him be peace and blessings, never
deviated from the Straight Path, and was always straightforward
in his deeds, words, and feelings. He guided the Companions,

---

[58] Al-Tirmidhi, "Tafsir al-Qur'an," 57.

who sought salvation and eternal happiness, to straightforwardness by saying: *Declare: "I have believed in God," and
then be straightforward*, a saying that concisely sums up all the
essential elements of belief and conduct.

If people claim progress on the path to the Truth, but are not
straightforward in their lives and conduct, all efforts will be in
vain, and they will have to account in the Hereafter for the time
spent without straightforwardness.[59] To reach the intended
destination, an initiate must be straightforward from the
beginning, maintain it throughout the journey, and be straightforward at the end of the path, as gratitude for being rewarded
with knowledge of God. Being alert to possible deviation in the
beginning, engaging in self-supervision during the journey, being
immune to incorrect thoughts and actions, and considering only
God's pleasure and approval in the end are significant signs of
this state:

> I know one among the people of straightforwardness:
> He was the most distinct in the realm of guidance.
> He sold his soul to the lights of (Divine) Identity,[60]
> And died purified of all the dirt of human nature.

A servant should seek straightforwardness, not wonder-
working or the power of spiritual unveiling or discovery. God
demands straightforwardness; however, a servant desires extraordinary spiritual abilities. When they told Bayazid al-Bistami
about a man who walked on water and flew in the air, he said:

> Fish and frogs also float on water, and insects and birds fly in the air.
> If you see a man float on his rug on water without sinking and sit
> cross-legged in the air, do not show any interest in him. Rather,
> consider whether he is straightforward in his state and conduct, and
> whether his actions are in accordance with the Sunna (the way of the
> Prophet, upon him be peace and blessings).[61]

---

[59] Muslim, "Iman," 62; Ibn Hanbal, *Musnad*, 3:413.

[60] In other words, he submitted himself wholly and without reserve to God.

[61] Al-Qushayri, *Al-Risala*, 397; Ahmad ibn 'Abd Allah Abu Nu'aym, *Hilyat al-
Awliya' wa Tabaqat al-Asfiya'*, 10 vols. (Beirut, 1967), 10:40.

What Bayazid advises is that a believer be straightforward and completely humble as a servant, rather than busying oneself working wonders.

Straightforwardness is the last step on a three-step stairway leading to nearness of God. The first step is consistency, where a traveler strives to embody Islam's theoretical and practical dimensions. Success in this continuous effort brings one's carnal self under control. The second step is settlement or tranquility, where an initiate purifies his or her inner self of the vices contaminating the spirit and heart (e.g., show, fame, and vanity, all of which cannot be reconciled with servanthood), thereby purging the heart of all that is not God. The third step is straightforwardness, where the doors of Divinity and creation are slightly opened to the traveler, and the Divine gifts are bestowed in the form of wonder-working and blessings, although he or she neither desires nor seeks them.

Straightforwardness, the last station on the way, means living without deviation from loyalty to God and under His direct protection; it is an environment in which Divine gifts and favors are bestowed. Flowers never fade away and hills and slopes do not experience winter, for it is an environment of eternal "spring." This is what is pointed out in: *If only they were straightforward on the path, then, assuredly We would give them to drink of "water" in abundance* (72:16). So long as people pursue straightforwardness on the path of belief in Divine Unity and fulfill their covenants with God and His Messenger by fulfilling the Divine ordinances, Divine gifts and bounties will flow abundantly.

Our master, upon him be peace and blessings, declares: *So long as the heart of a servant is not sound and straight, his belief cannot be true and upright; so long as his tongue is not true, his heart cannot be sound and straight.*[62] He also declares: *Every morning, the parts of a man's body warn his tongue, saying: "Fear God concerning us.*

---

[62] Ibn Hanbal, *Musnad*, 3:198.

For if you are true, we will be true and straight; if you are crooked, we will also deviate."[63]

Finally, let us hear a very significant warning from As'ad Mukhlis Pasha:

> Straightforwardness requires always being true and steadfast;
> Fix one of your legs in the center, and let "the free arm of the compass"
> [your other leg] travel around.[64]

---

[63] Al-Tirmidhi, "Zuhd," 61; Ibn Hanbal, *Musnad*, 3:96.

[64] In other words, one is to be well-grounded in Islam and to have good relations with all people in the world and call them to Islam. (Tr.)

Tawakkul (Reliance), Taslim (Surrender), Tafwiz (Commitment), and Thiqa (Confidence)

Tawakkul (Reliance), *Taslim* (Surrender), *Tafwiz* (Commitment), and *Thiqa* (Confidence) are the four steps or stations of a spiritual journey that begins with reliance on (or trust in) God, continuing in full awareness of one's helplessness and destitution before God, and ending in entrusting all of one's affairs to God Almighty in order to attain absolute peace and tranquillity of heart. Reliance (*tawakkul*) means total confidence in God, and feeling troubled or uneasy when it occurs to one that there may be other sources of power (that one can resort to). Without such a degree of confidence, it is wrong to talk about reliance. Moreover, one cannot attain reliance as long as the doors of the heart remain open to others.

Reliance means doing all that is necessary to obtain a desired or intended result, and then waiting in expectation for the Eternally-Powerful One to bring about His Will. Subsequent to this comes surrender (*taslim*), which many friends of God have described as being before God's Power and Will like a dead body in the hands of a mortician. Then comes commitment (*tafwiz*), leaving or committing all things and affairs to God and expecting everything from Him.

Reliance is the start of a journey, surrender is its end, and commitment is its result. Therefore, commitment has a wider meaning and relates to those who have almost completed the journey, rather than to beginners. Commitment comes after surrender, which requires the conviction of one's helplessness and destitution before God's Power and Wealth, and the ability to feel in one's heart the meaning of: *There is no power and strength save with God.* It also requires the utmost dependence on and the expectation of help from the heavenly treasure of: *There is no power and strength save with God.* In other words, commitment means that a traveler on the path of God is warned by his/her conscience, aware of the point of reliance and the point of seeking help, and in complete awareness of his or her helplessness and destitution, turns to the Unique Source of Power and Will and says: *Hold me by the hand, hold me, for I cannot do without You.*[65]

If reliance means that one entrusts all worldly and otherworldly affairs to the Lord, commitment means that one is fully aware that it is actually God Who does everything, Who produces every result, and Who creates all things and deeds that many consider to be done by themselves. Reliance means that one relies on God and closes the doors of one's heart to everything or everyone other than Him. It can be regarded as the outer fulfillment of all duties of worship and the inner attachment to God, the Lord Who is the sole Sustainer and Administrator of all that exists. This is what Shihab expresses in the following couplets:

> Rely on the All-Merciful in all your affairs;
> One who relies on Him is never at loss.
> Confide in God and be patient with His treatment of you,
> For you can obtain only as His favors what you expect from Him.

I think 'Umar, the second Caliph, may God be pleased with him, drew attention to the same point in a letter he wrote to Abu Musa al-'Ash'ari: *If you are able to submit to whatever or however God decrees for you [i.e. by not objecting to whatever befalls you], this is wholly good. If you are unable to do so, then endure it with patience.*

From another perspective, reliance signifies reliance on and

---

[65] Each person, by his or her very nature, feels two "impulses" or inner drives: the need for a source of help when helpless, and for a point of reliance when confronted with misfortune or the inability to fulfill his or her desires. God has placed these two innate impulses within each person so that He can be found during such personal crises. This fact is mentioned several times in the Qur'an, as in 10:22, which reminds people that when they are confronted with a storm (while at sea) from which there is no escape, they turn to God for help.

confidence in God. Surrender is the state of those who have been awakened to spiritual life. Commitment, meaning that travelers are not detained by considerations of means and causes, is a station special to those of high spiritual achievement.

Even if travelers possessing commitment seem to attach a certain importance to means and causes, this is due to the fact that they live in the material world, the sphere of means and causes, in which God has made any accomplishment dependent on certain preliminary conditions. If they give priority to means and causes, thereby disregarding the fact that God disposes of everything as He wishes, then they will become like vermin crawling on earth, despite their previous resemblance to birds flying in the heights of the heavens. It is related in books on the lives of saints that those saintly people who try to advance but become caught in the over-consideration of means and causes hear these words:

> Give up taking precautions,
> for involvement in precautions causes perishing;
> Commit your affairs to Us,
> for We are more thoughtful of you than yourself.

Such a commitment is a heroism that can be achieved only by those who persevere in their relations with God while living among people.

Doing what is necessary to obtain a certain result without attributing any creative effect to them may mean different things to different travelers: reliance for everybody, submission for those awakened to realities beyond the visible dimension, and commitment and confidence for those who have attained true peace or tranquillity of heart. How fine is the following saying of God's Messenger, upon him be peace and blessings, which combines exerting effort and reliance and commitment: *If you were able to rely on God as true reliance on Him requires, He would provide for you as He provides for birds that leave their nests hungry in the morning and return full in the evening.*[66]

---

[66] Al-Tirmidhi, "Zuhd," 33; Ibn Maja, "Zuhd," 14; Ibn Hanbal, *Musnad*, 1:30.

This Prophetic Tradition contains different truths for people of different spiritual ranks. What it means for the typical individual is what Rumi says:

> Even if reliance on God is a guide,
> Fulfilling preliminaries is a practice of the Prophet.
> He told (a Bedouin) loudly (in response to his question):
> *First fasten your camel and then rely on God.*

This meaning is what is pointed out in: *On God let the reliant rely* (14:12).

Those who lead their lives at the level of pure spirituality understand, in perfect awareness of their helplessness and weakness before God, that they should trust wholly in God's Power and Strength, and become like a corpse in the hands of a mortician: *In God put your trust, if you are true believers* (5:23). As for those who fly around the summits of "self-annihilation in God" and "subsistence with God," they say, like Prophet Abraham, upon him be peace, even while being thrown into fire: *God is sufficient for me* (39:38) and commit their affairs wholly to Him. It is enough for them that God Almighty knows their condition.

We can also see this greatest degree of commitment in God's Messenger, upon him be peace and blessings. When the feet of those pursuing him during his emigration to Madina were seen from the cave where he was hiding with his nearest friend Abu Bakr, may God be pleased with him, and their pursuers' voices echoed from the cave's walls, he relied wholly upon God and told Abu Bakr: *Grieve not! Assuredly, God is with us* (9:40). This is also alluded to in the verse: *Whoever puts his trust in God, He will suffice him* (65:3).

Commitment and confidence are the highest degrees of reliance on God. Those who have attained these degrees have entirely submitted their reason, logic, and belief, as well as their outer and inner feelings, to God's commandments. As a result, they have become "polished mirrors" in which His Names, Attributes, and acts are reflected. Signs of these degrees are understanding that taking precautions is included in God's preordainment, and thereby finding peace; seeing their willpower as a dim shadow of the Divine Will, and turning to that Divine Will; and being pleased with God's treatment, whether it be favorable or not, and agreeing with whatever happens to them.

The author of *Minhaj* describes this degree of commitment as follows:

> I committed all my affairs to the Dear One,
> Whether He keeps me alive or makes me die.

The following words of Wasif of Andarun are also most appropriate:

> Whatever was destined will certainly happen, so
> Commit your affairs to God; neither be grieved nor suffer pains.

One of the most beautiful descriptions of commitment belongs to Ibrahim Haqqi, the initial verses of whose *Tafwiznama* (Description of Tafwiz) are as follows:

> God changes evils into good;
> Never think that He does otherwise.
> One with knowledge of Him watches
> In admiration what He does.
> Let us see what our Master does;
> He does well whatever He does.
> Put your trust in God, the Truth;
> And commit to Him your affairs
> So that you may find peace.
> Be patient and agree (with whatever He does).
> Let us see what our Master does;
> He does well whatever He does.

Khuluq (Good Nature)

Khuluq (good nature), in addition to meaning temperament, disposition, and character, is a goal to which a traveler aspires, for it is the most important dimension of creation. In brief, this station means that one is characterized (equipped) with God's qualities or way of acting. For example, God is All-Forgiving; therefore, one must be forgiving. One who realizes this sacred goal can easily perform all good acts or deeds.

The words *khalq* (creation) and *khuluq* (nature) are derived from the same root word. *Khalq* relates to the external form or appearance, the visible, material, and experienced dimension of existence; *khuluq* is concerned with the spiritual dimension, meaning, or content. An individual cannot be judged or known by his or her outer appearance, for one's real identity lies in one's character, temperament, and natural disposition. No matter how many different images one may project, one's true character or temperament will eventually reveal itself. How meaningful are the following words of an Arab poet of the pre-Islamic Age of Ignorance:

> If a man has a bad quality, sooner or later it will reveal itself;
> Let him continue to think that it can remain hidden.

In other words, the outer appearance is deceiving, for one's natural disposition removes or corrects all deceptions and thereby reveals one's true nature. Since one may acquire a second nature through education and habituation, moralists divide nature into good and bad. In the present context, we use "nature" to mean "good nature."

The most accurate standard of a good spiritual life, one that Sufism uses to describe or qualify a person, is good nature. One who has taken a few steps forward in good nature may be regarded as advanced in the spiritual life. Although miracles, dazzling stations, and superhuman actions may be acceptable when they issue from good nature, they are worthless if not combined with good nature.

When asked which believer was better on account of his or her belief, Prophet Muhammad, upon him be peace and blessings, answered: *The one who is better in conduct or nature.*[67] This is natural, because God praises and consoles His most distinguished servant Prophet Muhammad, upon him be peace and blessings, not with His extraordinary favors but with his laudable virtues and praiseworthy qualities, declaring: *You stand on an exalted standard of character* (68:4). His nature was the aim and fruit of his creation. Since the Prophet's conduct embodied Islam and the Qur'an, when his wife 'A'isha, may God be pleased with her, was asked about his conduct by Sa'id ibn Hisham, she answered: *Do you not read the Qur'an? His conduct is (the embodiment of) the Qur'an.*[68]

The verse: *You stand on an exalted standard of character* (68:4) shows that the incomparable conduct of the Prophet was based on the Qur'an. In addition to his outer and inner faculties and senses, and the material and immaterial aspects of his creation and character, the Prophet, upon him be peace and blessings, was endowed with all the characteristics needed to be the most advanced and greatest representative of human virtue. Developing these potentials to the highest degree possible, he attained the highest degree of human perfection.

Not content with this state, as is declared in the verse: *Surely, in the Messenger of God you have a good example for him who hopes for God and the Last Day, and remembers God much* (33:21), he established the most excellent example for his followers and thereby gradually transformed them into the most virtuous community of all time. With such sayings as: *The most*

---

[67] Sulayman ibn Ash'as al-Sijistani Abu Dawud, *Sunan Abi Dawud*, 4 vols. (Beirut, n.d.), 14; Ibn Hanbal, *Musnad*, 2:250.

[68] Muslim, "Musafirin," 139.

perfect in belief among the believers are the most perfect in conduct[69]; A man can "cross" with good conduct the "distances" which he cannot with acts of worship and adoration[70]; and: *The first virtue to be weighed in the Balance (in the other world) is good conduct,*[71] and by employing the perfect, fruitful principles he brought to perfect humanity, he guided his followers to the realms where angels dwell.

The indications of having a good nature have been summarized as follows: a person possessing this quality does not hurt anybody by either word or deed, overlooks those who hurt him or her and forgives the evils done, and reciprocates evil with good. The Prophet, upon him be peace and blessings, who is praised with the verse: *You stand on an exalted standard of character* (68:4), is the most excellent example of these virtues. He was not offended by the one who stood before him and told him to be just,[72] by the one who pulled his robe from the back and hurt him,[73] by the one who threw dust on his head and insulted him, or by the one who slandered his innocent and beloved wife, 'A'isha.[74] In fact, he visited each of these individuals when they became ill[75] and attended their funeral processions.[76] He did so because good nature was a dimension of his blessed existence.

Many people seem to be good natured, mild-mannered, and humane, although good conduct and mildness are no more than affectations. When they experience a little irritation, anger, or harsh treatment, their true nature is revealed. One

---

[69] Abu Dawud, *Sunan*, 14; Ibn Hanbal, *Musnad*, 2:250.

[70] Al-Haythami, *Majma' al-Zawa'id*, 8:24.

[71] 'Ala al-Din 'Ali al-Muttaqi al-Hindi, *Kanz al-'Ummal fi Sunan al-Aqwal wa al-Af'al*, 8 vols. (Beirut: 1985), hadith no. 5160.

[72] Al-Bukhari, "Adab," 95; Muslim, "Zakat," 142.

[73] Al-Bukhari, "Khumus," 19; Muslim, "Zakat," 142.

[74] Al-Bukhari, "Shahada," 15; Muslim, "Tawba," 56.

[75] Abu Dawud, "Jana'iz," 1.

[76] Al-Bukhari, "Tafsir Sura 9," 12; Muslim, "Munafiqun," 3.

who has a good nature does not change his or her manners even when in a hellish state, but remains mild and shows no harshness. A heart open to good nature is like a very broad space to bury one's anger and rage. Those intolerant and impatient ones who display bad conduct, are like Cain, more stupid than the raven, and can find no place to bury their anger, hatred, and ill feelings.

Let us conclude this discussion with the following couplet:

It is by good nature that a man can be perfected;
It is by good nature that the order of the world is maintained.

Tawadu (Humility)

*Tawadu (*modesty and humility) is the opposite of arrogance, pride, and haughtiness. It can also be interpreted as one's awareness of one's real position before God, and as letting that realization guide one's conduct toward God and with people. If one sees oneself as an ordinary, individual part of creation, a threshold of a door, a mat spread on a floor or a paving stone, a pebble in a stream or chaff in a field, and if one can sincerely confess, as did Muhammad Lutfi Effendi: *Everybody else is good but I am bad; everybody else is wheat but I am chaff,* the inhabitants of the heavens will kiss him or her on the head.

In a narration attributed to the truthful, confirmed one, upon him be peace and blessings, it is said: *Whoever is humble, God exalts him; whoever is haughty, God humiliates him.*[77] Thus, one's true greatness is inversely proportional to one's arrogance, just as one's true smallness is inversely proportional to one's humility.

Humility has been defined in many ways: seeing oneself as being devoid of all virtues that originate in oneself, treating others humbly and respectfully, seeing oneself as the worst of humanity (unless being honored by special Divine treatment), and being alert to any stirring of the ego and immediately suppressing it. Each definition expresses a dimension of humility. However, the last definition relates to those made sincere by God Himself, those who are near to Him.

A Companion saw Caliph 'Umar, may God be pleased with him, carrying water in a pitcher on his shoulder. He asked him: *What are you doing, O Caliph of God's Messenger?* 'Umar, one

---

[77] Al-Haythami, *Majma' al-Zawa'id,* 10:325.

of the foremost in nearness to God, answered: *Some envoys have come from other countries. I felt some conceit in my heart and wanted to suppress it.* 'Umar used to carry flour on his back.[78] Once, while giving a sermon from the pulpit, he blamed himself for an action, keeping silent when people questioned and criticized his action.

Abu Hurayra carried wood while he was the deputy governor of Madina.[79] When he was the chief judge in Madina, Zayd ibn Thabit kissed Ibn 'Abbas' hand, and Ibn 'Abbas, known as the Interpreter of the Qur'an and the Scholar of the Umma, helped Zayd get on his horse.[80] Hasan, the grandson of the Prophet, upon him be peace and blessings, sat with some children who were eating bread crumbs and ate with them. Once Abu Dharr offended Bilal al-Habashi and, to obtain his forgiveness, put his head on the ground and declared: *If the blessed feet of Bilal do not tread on this sinful head, it will not rise from the ground.* All of these events and many similar ones are instances of humility.

Both God Almighty and His Messenger emphasized humility so much that one who is aware of this can not doubt that servanthood consists of humility. The Qur'anic verse: *The servants of the All-Merciful are those who walk on the earth in modesty, and if the impudent offend them, they continue their way saying: "Peace"* (25:63) praises humility, and the Divine statements *extremely humble toward believers* (5:54) and *merciful among themselves; you find them bowing down and falling prostrate* (48:29) are expressions of praise for the ingrained humility reflected in their conduct.

Concerning humility, the glory of humanity, upon him be peace and blessings, declared: *God has told me that you must be*

---

[78] 'Izz al-Din Abu al-Hasan 'Ali ibn Muhammad al-Jazari Ibn al-Athir, *Usd al-Ghaba fi Ma'rifat al Sahaba*, 8 vols. (Cairo, 1970), 4:165.

[79] Abu al-Fida' Isma'il Ibn Kathir, *Al-Bidaya wa al-Nihaya*, 14 vols. (Beirut: Maktabat al-Ma'arif, 1966), 8:113.

[80] Ibn Hajar al Asqalani, *Al-Isaba fi Tamyiz al-Sahaba*, 4 vols. (Beirut: 1238 AH / 1910 CE), 2:332.

humble, and that no one must boast to another[81]; Shall I inform you of one whom Hellfire will not touch? Hellfire will not touch one who is near to God and amiable with people, and mild and easy to get along with[82]; God exalts one who is humble. That one sees himself as small while he is truly great in the sight of people[83]; and O God, make me see myself as small.[84]

The glory of humanity, upon him be peace and blessings, lived as the most humble of people. He stopped at the places where children were gathered, greeted them, and played with them.[85] If someone held him by the hand and wanted to lead him somewhere, he never objected.[86] He helped his wives with the housework.[87] When people were working, he worked with them.[88] He mended his shoes and clothes, milked sheep, and fed animals.[89] He sat at the table with his servant.[90] He always welcomed the poor warmly, looked after widows and orphans,[91] visited the ill, attended funerals, and answered the call of slaves in his community.[92]

The beloved servants of God, from God's Messenger, upon him be peace and blessings, to Caliph 'Umar and the Umayyad Caliph 'Umar ibn 'Abd al-'Aziz and from him to numerous saints, purified and perfected scholars, and those honored with nearness to God,

---

[81] Muslim, "Janna," 64; Abu Dawud, "Adab," 40.

[82] Al-Tirmidhi, "Sifat al-Qiyama," 45.

[83] Abu Nu'aym, *Hilyat al-Awliya'*, 7:129.

[84] Muslim, "Zuhd," 14.

[85] Al-Bukhari, "Isti'dhan," 15; Muslim, "Salam," 15.

[86] Abu al-Fida Qadi 'Iyad, *Al-Shifa' al-Sharif*, 2 vols. (Beirut: Dar al Fikr, 1988), 1:131.

[87] Al-Bukhari, "Nafaqat," 8; Al-Tirmidhi, "Sifat al-Qiyama," 45.

[88] Ibn Hanbal, *Musnad*, 2:383; Muhammad Ibn Hisham, *Al-Sira al-Nabawiya*, 9 vols. (Beirut: Dar al-Ihya' al-Turath al-'Arabi, n.d.), 2:141.

[89] Al-Tirmidhi, Shama'il," 78; Ibn Hanbal, *Musnad*, 6:256.

[90] Al-Bukhari, "At'ima," 55; Muslim, "Ayman," 42.

[91] Al-Bukhari, "Nafaqat," 1; "Talaq," 25; Muslim, "Zuhd," 41, 42.

[92] Al-Bukhari, Tafsir Sura 9, 12; Muslim, Munafiqin, 3.

have held that the signs of greatness in the great are humility and modesty, while the signs of pettiness in the petty are arrogance and vanity. Based on this understanding, these great people sought to show men and women how to become perfect.

True humility means that people must know the full extent of their worth before God's infinite Grandeur, and then make this fully realized potential an ingrained, essential part of their nature. Those who have done this are humble and balanced in their relations with others. Those who have realized their nothingness before God Almighty are balanced in both their religious lives and their relations with people. They obey the commandments of religion, for they have no objection to the revealed truths of religion, nor do they criticize its method of addressing or relating to human reason. They are convinced that what is contained in the Qur'an and the authentic Traditions of the Prophet, upon him be peace and blessings, is true.

If there is an apparent contradiction between these two sources and human reason or established rational or scientific facts, such people seek to learn the truth of the matter. Therefore, it is nonsense for those without humility and modesty to assert, when confronted with an apparent contradiction between reason or rational premises and the revealed and narrated principles of religion, that reason or what is rational must be preferred. Their further assertion that judgments based on reasoning and analogy must be given priority over revealed principles is also mistaken. The wonders worked and spiritual pleasures felt by following ways not followed by the Prophet, upon him be peace and blessings, is God's way of leading to perdition as their merits, for "success" in such endeavors leads to sin.

Those who have achieved humility are completely convinced of the truth of whatever the Prophet said or did, upon him be peace and blessings. They never doubt it, and seek to practice it in their lives. If something else, such as a wise saying or a great accomplishment, appears to them as more beautiful or acceptable, they accuse themselves of being unable to discern the incomparable superiority of the revealed truths and expressions, saying:

> There are many people who find fault with words that have no fault.
> However, the fault lies in their defective understanding.

They are certain that one cannot prosper in the Hereafter by following ways opposed to the Qur'an and the Sunna. They find the greatest source of power in servanthood to God. In reality, one who worships God never adores anyone else, and one who serves others cannot be a true servant of God. How apt are the following words of Bediuzzaman:

> Do not see anything or anybody else other than God as much greater than you as to deserve adoration or servanthood. Do not boast of yourself in a way to see yourself as greater than others. As creatures are equally distant from being worshipped, so also are they equal in that they have all been created.

Those who are truly humble do not attribute the fruits of their work and efforts to themselves, nor do they regard any success or effort on the way of God as making them superior to others. They do not care how other people regard them, and do not demand a return for their services on the way of God. They regard their being loved by others as a test of their sincerity,[93] and do not exploit God's favors to them by boasting to others about them.

In short, just as humility is the portal to good conduct or being characterized with the qualities of God (such as generosity, mercy, helpfulness, forgiveness, and so on), it is also the first and foremost means of being near to both the created and the Creator. Roses grow on the earth, and humanity was created on the earth, not in the heavens. A believer is nearest to God when prostrating before Him. While recounting the Prophet's Ascension to the heavens, the Qur'an refers to him as God's servant, as a sign of his humility and utmost modesty.

---

[93] In other words, they view other people's love for them as the reason for doing good deeds, not as a way of asserting their superiority over others.

Futuwwa (Youth and Chivalry)

Futuwwa, defined as youth and chivalry, is really a composite of such virtues as generosity, munificence, modesty, chastity, trustworthiness, loyalty, mercifulness, knowledge, humility, and piety. It is a station on the path to God as well as a dimension of sainthood, and also signifies that altruism and helping others have become one's second nature. It is an important, indispensable dimension of good conduct and a significant aspect of humanity.

Derived from *fata'* (young man), *futuwwa* has become a symbol of rebellion against all evil and the endeavor for sincere servanthood to God:

> They were young men who had believed in their Lord, and We increased them in guidance. And We strengthened their hearts, when they rose up and declared: *Our Lord is the Lord of the heavens and Earth; we will not call upon any god beside Him, or then we had spoken an outrage.* (18:14)

expresses this eloquently. They said: *We have heard a youth talk of them (the idols); he is called Abraham* (21:60) expresses the position and influence of one who has achieved perfect *futuwwa* in his or her community, one who has sought to guide humanity to truth. By contrast, the young men mentioned in the verses: *With him there came into the prison two young men* (12:36) and: *(Joseph) told his young (servants) to put their merchandise (with which they had bartered) into their saddle-bags* (12:62) were ordinary young men without chivalry.

As many people have written on or talked about *futuwwa* since the Age of Happiness, the concept has been defined in many ways: not despising the poor or being deceived by the rich and riches; being fair to everybody without expecting fairness in return; living one's life as a pitiless enemy of one's carnal self; being ever-considerate of others and living for them; smashing all idols or all that is idolized, and rebelling against falsehood so as to be wholly devoted to God Almighty; bearing whatever evil is done to oneself, but roaring when the rights of God are violated; feeling remorse for the rest of one's life for committing the smallest of sins, but overlooking others' sins, regardless of how large they are; seeing oneself as a poor, lowly servant while considering others as saintly; not resenting others while maintaining relations with those who resent you; being kind to those who hurt you; serving God and the people before everyone else, but putting others first when it is time to receive one's rewards.

Some have summed up *futuwwa* in the four virtues mentioned by Haydar Karrar 'Ali, the fourth Caliph and cousin of the Prophet, upon him be peace and blessings,. They are: forgiving when one is able to punish, preserving mildness and acting mildly and gently when one is angry, wishing one's enemies well and doing good to them, and being considerate of others' well-being and happiness first, even when one is needy.

'Ali was one of the greatest representatives of *futuwwa*. When he was stabbed by Ibn Muljam while leading the morning prayer in the mosque, his children, who saw that their father was going to die, asked him what he wanted them to do to Ibn Muljam. He did not order his execution in retaliation.[94] During a battle, 'Ali threw his enemy to the ground and then released him. His reason was: When 'Ali was about to kill this man, the latter spat in 'Ali's face, which angered him. Fearing that his motive for killing the man was now confused and sullied, 'Ali released him.[95] He felt sincere grief when Zubayr ibn 'Awwam, a leading Companion and his enemy in the Battle of the Camel, was killed.[96] Since he always considered others first, even when he

---

[94] Ibn al-Athir, *Usd al-Ghaba*, 4:118.

[95] Shamsaddin Sivasi, *Manaqib Jiharyar Guzin*, 258.

[96] Al-Haythami, *Majma' al-Zawa'id*, 9:150.

was in need, he usually wore summer clothes in winter and trembled with cold.[97] It was said about him that there could be no young, chivalrous man like 'Ali, and there could be no sword like Dhu al-Fiqar ('Ali's sword).[98] 'Ali lived with the Prophet, upon him be peace and blessings, and was raised by him. He lived a perfectly honest, pure life without any stain, and embodied God's answer to Prophet Moses, upon him be peace, about *futuwwa*: *It means that you are able to return your self to Me as pure or untainted as you received it from Me.*

The signs of a *fata'* (young, chivalrous one) are that the individual, created with the potential to accept Divine Unity and Islam, is totally convinced of the Divine Unity; this urges him or her to live according to the requirements of this conviction; that, without being captivated by carnal or bodily desires, he or she lives a pure, spiritual life; and that he or she always seeks to please God in his or her deeds, thoughts, and feelings. One who cannot be saved from the temptations of the carnal self, Satan, appetites, love of the world, or attachment to the worldly life cannot climb upward to the peak of *futuwwa*.

> *Futuwwa* is a treasure obtainable by climbing high beyond
> all the "highest mountains of the world";
> What business have those who fall tired
> even on a smooth road with such a treasure?

---

[97] Ibid., 9:122.

[98] 'Ali al-Qari, *Al-Asrar al-Marfu'a fi akhbar al-Mawdu'a* (Beirut, 1986), 367.

Sidq (Truthfulness)

Meaning true thoughts, true words and true actions, *sidq* is reflected in the life of a traveler on the path to God as follows: he or she does not lie, lives according to truthfulness, and strives to be a trustworthy representative of loyalty to God. In other words, he or she never deviates from truthfulness in all thoughts, words and actions and, in obedience to the Qur'anic command: *Be with the truthful* (9:119), always seeks truthfulness on both an individual and a social level. Such people are so careful about being truthful that they never give false evidence or tell lies even in jest. As related in a Prophetic saying, one who is truthful to that degree is recorded as a truthful one by the Supreme Court, while one whose thoughts, words, and actions are contradictory and who deceives others is recorded as a liar.[99]

Truthfulness is the most reliable road leading to God, and the truthful are fortunate travelers upon it. Truthfulness is the spirit and essence of action and the genuine standard of straightforwardness in thought; it distinguishes believers from hypocrites, and the people of Paradise from the people of the Fire. Truthfulness is a Prophetic virtue in those who are not Prophets, by which "servants" share the same blessings as "kings." In the Qur'an, God Almighty described as being true both the one who communicated the Qur'an and the one who confirmed it: *He who came with the truth and he who declared that it is true* (39:33).

Truthfulness can be defined as struggling to preserve one's integrity and to avoid hypocrisy and lying, even in difficult circumstances when a lie will bring about salvation. Junayd al-Baghdadi says: *A loyal, truthful one changes states at least*

---

[99] Al-Bukhari, "Adab," 69; Muslim, "Birr," 103-5; Abu Dawud, "Adab," 80.

forty times a day (in order to preserve personal integrity), while a hypocrite remains the same for forty years without feeling any trouble or unease (over his or her deviation).[100]

The initial and lowest degree of truthfulness is sincerity and behaving the same whether in public or in private. This is followed by being true in all thoughts, feelings, actions, and intentions. The truthful are those valiant people whose feelings, thoughts, and actions do not contradict one another; the most truthful are those heroes who are absolutely true in all of their fantasy, intentions, feelings, thoughts, actions, and gestures.

Using all of one's faculties and capacities to achieve truthfulness in all actions, loyalty to a lofty ideal or cause, and steadfastness in pursuing it is an attribute of Prophethood. In the verse: *Make mention of Abraham in the Book: he was a most truthful one, a Prophet* (19:41), the Qur'an refers to this highest degree of truthfulness. Truthfulness is the primary attribute of all Prophets, and the strongest moral force or means-producing activity for serving Islam and the Qur'an. It is also a believer's greatest credit and most valid document in the Hereafter. God draws our attention to this significant fact: *This is a day in which their truthfulness profits the truthful* (5:119).

Truthfulness serves the Prophets, the purified and perfected scholars and the saints brought near to God as a heavenly mount that, as quick as lightning, can carry them to the highest heights; lying, however, pulls Satan and his followers down to the lowest depths. Thoughts "fly upward" on the wings of truthfulness and increase in value, actions grow and flourish on the ground of truthfulness, and only true and sincere supplications and prayers reach the Throne of Mercy and are welcomed.

Truthfulness is as effective as the "elixir" of God's Greatest Name. When asked about the Greatest Name, Bayazid al-Bistami answered:

---

[100] Al-Qushayri, *Al-Risala*, 211.

Show me the Least Name among God's Names so that I may show
you the Greatest One. If there is something as effective (for the
acceptability by God of prayers and actions) as the Greatest Name, it
is truthfulness. Whichever Name is recited truthfully, It becomes the
Greatest.[101]

Truthfulness caused the light of repentance to shine on the
forehead of Prophet Adam, upon him be peace. Truthfulness
served as a vessel of salvation for Prophet Noah, upon him be
peace, when the world was flooded. Truthfulness carried
Prophet Abraham, upon him be peace, to safety and coolness
from the fire into which he had been thrown. Truthfulness
elevates ordinary people to extraordinary heights, and is a key
that opens the door to realms and realities beyond visible
existence. One borne aloft by truthfulness cannot be detained
from journeying upward, and doors are not closed in the face
of one who uses this key. How apt are the words of Rumi in
this respect:

> The truthfulness of a lover affects even the lifeless;
> Why then should it be found strange that it affects man's heart?
> The truthfulness of Moses affected his staff and the mountain;
> Nay, it also affected that great, splendid sea.
> As for the truthfulness of Muhammad, it affected
> The beautiful face of the Moon and also the shining Sun.[102]

In many verses, the Qur'an relates that being a true believer
depends upon one's integrity and truthfulness in words, actions,

---

[101] Abu Nu'aym, *Hilyat al-Awliya'*, 10:39. Note: All of God's Names are great.
But, with respect to comprehending manifestation and inclusiveness, some
may be greater than others. For example, God, the Proper Name of the Divine
Being, is the most comprehensive of all and includes all other Names. This is
also true of the name the All-Merciful, which is considered as almost
synonymous with God. According to the mission and function of each, which
Name is the greatest varies among the Prophets and saints. For example, the
Greatest Name for Prophet Jesus was the All-Powerful (according to Muhy al-
Din ibn al-'Arabi) and the All-Speaking for Prophet Moses, peace be upon
them both.

[102] Rumi alludes to Moses' staff changing into a snake (20:20) and his using it
to part the sea (26:63), and to the splitting of the Moon into two by a gesture of
Prophet Muhammad, upon him be peace and blessings, with his finger (54:1).

feelings, and innermost senses. It also regards such a degree of integrity and truthfulness as the basis of happiness in both this world and the next. The following are a few examples:

· *Say: My Lord, cause me to enter with truth, and cause me to go out with truth, and grant me a power from Your Presence to help me.* (17:80)

· *Grant me a good reputation, being remembered for truthfulness, in later generations.* (26:84)

· *Give to those who believe good tidings that they have a true, sure footing in the sight of their Lord.* (10:2)

· *The truthful are in the Gardens and rivers, on the seats of truthfulness in the Presence of a Mighty King.* (54:54-5)

Entering with truth, going out with truth, being remembered for truthfulness, true and sure footing, and a seat of truthfulness are all stations of and provisions for a long road extending from this world to the Hereafter. Since what takes place in this world yields fruit in the Hereafter, the truthful always pursue what is true, observe truthfulness when starting a task or moving to another place in the way of God, act and live in accord with the requirements of truthfulness, and bequeath truthfulness to succeeding generations. Their objective is to deserve eternal happiness in the Hereafter.

To become truthful in intentions and aims, believers must consciously decide to become truthful in their thoughts, decisions, and acts. This is the first step. Those so resolved must persist in truthfulness, regardless of the consequences, and refrain from whatever might shake their resolution. The second step is to maintain this worldly life only to support the truth and gain God's approval and pleasure. Such people are always aware of the defects and faults of their selfhood, and do not surrender to the world's attractions and change their conditions for worldly reasons. The third step is to establish truthfulness so firmly in one's conscience that it governs every facet of life. This is identical with the station of being pleased, which is explained in the Tradition: *One who is pleased with God as the Lord and Islam as the religion and Muhammad as the Prophet has tasted the delight of belief.*[103]

The greatest truthfulness and loyalty is for people to be pleased with the Lordship of God regardless of the treatment He dispenses, to accept Islam as the Divine system governing their lives, and to submit willingly to the guidance or leadership of the best of creation, upon him be peace and blessings. The way to true humanity lies in undertaking this grave responsibility, which is a difficult one to fulfill perfectly.

Let us conclude with a fine couplet:

> What befits man is truthfulness even if under threat;
> God Almighty is the helper of the truthful.

---

[103] Muslim, "Iman," 56; Nasa'i, "Jihad," 18.

Haya (Modesty)

Sufis use *haya*, which literally means shame, bashfulness, and refraining from saying or doing anything improper or indecent, to describe one who, out of fear and awe of God, seeks to avoid displeasing Him. It urges one to be more careful, self-possessed, and self-controlled, for such restraint, if originating in feelings of modesty, results in giving God the respect He deserves. If these feelings are absent or lost due to familial or environmental influences, it will be difficult to develop them.

In the light of the explanations above, modesty can be divided into two categories: an innate or instinctive feeling of shame, which prevents people from engaging in what is considered shameful and indecent, and modesty originating in belief, which constitutes an important, deep dimension of Islam.

Combining an instinctive feeling of shame with the modesty based on Islam forms the greatest safeguard against shameful or indecent acts. Alone, each one may be diminished or utterly lost. If this innate feeling of shame is not combined with an awareness that comes from belief, expressed in verses like: *Does he not know that God sees (all things)?* (96:14), and a consciousness of God's constant vigil over us: *God is ever watching over you* (4:1), it cannot last long, for its endurance depends on belief. This essential relation between modesty and belief was expressed by God's Messenger, who told a Companion after hearing his advice concerning modesty to another man: *Leave him, for modesty comes from belief.*[104] He also said: *Belief has seventy or so divisions. Modesty is a division of belief.*[105]

---

[104] Al-Bukhari, "Iman," 16; Muslim, "Iman," 59; Abu Dawud, "Adab," 6.

[105] Abu Dawud, "Sunna," 14; Nasa'i, "Iman," 16.

We may conclude from these Prophetic sayings that, like other seeds of innate virtues, one's natural feeling of shame can develop to the extent by which it is strengthened with the forces and means that produce knowledge of God. It then becomes a dimension of one's spiritual life, an obstacle against the carnal self's excessive desires. If this feeling is not reinforced and developed with belief and knowledge of God or strengthened with consciousness of God's constant vigil, and is left to dissipate in sensual or carnal pleasure, one will witness in an individual or a community the development of those indecencies and perversions that make anyone truly human ashamed of being human. The glory of humankind and the perfect example of modesty, upon him be peace and blessings, said: *If you have no modesty, do whatever you wish.*[106]

The words *haya* (modesty or feeling of shame) and *hayat* (life) come from the same root. This signifies that modesty is an indication of a lively heart, and that a heart's liveliness depends on its owner's belief and knowledge of God. If a heart is not fed continuously with belief and knowledge of God, it is almost impossible for it to remain lively to and give rise to modesty.

According to Junayd al-Baghdadi, *haya* means awareness of the material and immaterial bounties bestowed by God, and consciousness of personal defects and faults. Dhu al-Nun al-Misri holds that *haya* means that one constantly feels shame in his or her heart on account of personal sins and offenses, and is therefore careful about his or her actions.[107] Another spiritual master defines *haya* as never forgetting how God treats one and ordering one's life according to the fact that God knows all actions and thoughts.

It is recorded in al-Qushayri's *Al-Risala* that God declares: *O son of Adam! So long as you maintain your modesty and feeling of shame before Me, I make people forget your defects.*[108] The

---

[106] Al-Buhkari, "Anbiya'," 54; Abu Dawud, "Adab," 6; Ibn Maja, "Zuhd," 17.
[107] Al-Qushayri, *Al-Risala*, 215.
[108] Ibid., 216.

Lord of Might and Dignity also said to Jesus, upon him be peace: *O Jesus, first advise your own selfhood. If it accepts your advice, then you may advise others, or else you must feel ashamed of yourself before Me.*[109]

Some have mentioned different categories of modesty or shame. For example, the shame or modesty felt by:

· Adam, who felt guilty until he was forgiven.

· The angels for their heartfelt incapacity to give due worship to God, as expressed in their saying: *Glory be to You! We are unable to worship You as Your worship requires*, although they glorify Him day and night without stopping.

· Gnostics or those distinguished with knowledge of God in the face of His Majesty, despite their profound knowledge of Him, which they express as: *Glory be to You! We are unable to know You as Your knowledge requires.*

· The spiritually advanced when in awe of God, even though they never give in to their carnal desires and ambitions.

· Those distinguished with utmost conviction of God because of their supposed distance from Him, though they always feel His infinite nearness despite the infinite distance of humanity from God Almighty

· Lovers of God who feel disloyalty arising from their anxiety over not being able to love God as His love requires.

· Those who feel a lack of sufficient sincerity and do not know for what they must pray to God.

· Those exalted ones who are conscious of the fact that they, as human beings, have been honored with the fairest creation, because of the base acts of which they accuse themselves of and which, according to them, are irreconcilable with being part of the fairest creation.

---

[109] Ibid.

The first degree of modesty is to see oneself with the sight of God. That is, one practices self-control or self-supervision according to God's standards. This practice engenders a feeling of shame or modesty that produces extreme caution in thoughts and acts. Such a degree of modesty is found in people considered alive in feelings and thoughts.

The second degree is proportional to one's awareness of what nearness to God and always being in His Presence mean. This can be experienced by those who are always conscious of the meaning of: *He is with you wherever you may be* (57:4), about which the Prophet, upon him be peace and blessings, said:

> Be as modest before God Almighty as the necessity of being modest before Him requires. Let him who is blessed with this degree of modesty always control his mind and its contents, as well as his stomach and its contents. Let him always remember that death and decay follow. One who desires the afterlife will renounce the adornments of the world. One who is able to do that can feel as much modesty before God as being modest before Him requires.[110]

One can reach the third degree by deeply feeling the absolute Divine disposal of all things, by living a life of profound spirituality in pursuit of the final destination: *And in your Lord is the final goal* (53:42). The effort to reach this final goal continues throughout a whole life dedicated to following the path to Him.

One's degree of modesty determines one's true humanity. If a traveler cannot order his or her life and discipline his or her acts according to the demands of the eternal life and to live in utmost humility and modesty, then his or her existence is a personal shame and a burden to others, as stated in the following couplet:

> By God, there is good neither in life
> Nor in the world when modesty disappears.

Modesty is a Divine quality and mystery. If people knew to Whom it essentially relates, they would act more carefully and sensitively. To illuminate this point, it is related that

---

[110] Ibn Hanbal, *Musnad*, 1:387.

God Almighty asks an old man on the Place of Resurrection to account for his acts in the world: *Why did you commit such and such sins?* The old man denies that he did so. So, the Most Compassionate of the Compassionate commands the angels: *Take him to Paradise.* The angels want to know why the Almighty has commanded so, even though He knows that the old man committed those sins. The Almighty answers: *I know, but I looked at his white beard as one belonging to the Community of Muhammad and felt ashamed to tell him that I knew he was lying.*[111]

As recorded in *Kanz al-'Ummal*, when the Archangel Gabriel told this to God's Messenger, upon him be peace and blessings, the Messenger's eyes filled with tears and he said regretfully:

God Almighty feels ashamed to punish those of my Community whose beards have turned white, but those of my Community with white beards do not feel ashamed to commit sins.[112]

To sum up:

Hayiy (All-Modest) is one of the Divine Names,
So strive and acquire modesty.

---

[111] Justice requires that good deeds be rewarded and evil deeds punished. Although God is not accountable for what He does and how He does it, He is absolutely just and compassionate. He is not compelled to do or not to do anything. In theory, God can send to Hell a believer who did good deeds and to Paradise an unbeliever who always did wrong. This does not mean that God does so; it only expresses God's absolute Will and Freedom. God sends to Paradise a believer who did good deeds and to Hell an unbeliever. This is His justice. One can enter Paradise only by God's compassion and forgiveness. As one cannot be thankful enough even for one of his or her eyes, how could he or she be thankful enough to merit Heaven due to his or her deeds? Even a whole life spent in devotion to God would not be enough. God enables one to do good deeds. The Prophet, upon him be peace and blessings, declares: *No one, including me, can go to Paradise by his deeds, unless God has enveloped me in His mercy.* Muslim scholars have concluded that Paradise is purely out of mercy, while Hell is out of justice. Another point is that God (usually) forgives and has mercy on those entitled to it by belief and good deeds. If one is sent to Hell, it (usually) means that he or she has received what he or she deserves.

[112] Al-Muttaqi al-Hindi, *Kanz al-'Ummal*, hadith no. 42680.

Shukr (Thankfulness)

Literally meaning gladness felt about and gratitude shown for the good done to one, Sufis use *shukr* to mean using one's body, abilities, feelings, and thoughts bestowed upon one to fulfill the purpose of his or her creation: being thankful to the Creator for what He has bestowed. Such thankfulness is to be reflected in a person's actions or daily life, in speech and in the heart, by admitting that all things come directly from Him, and by feeling gratitude for them.

One may thank God in words only by depending upon His Power and Strength, as well as upon His bestowal or withholding of favors, and acknowledging that all good and bounties come from Him. As He alone creates all good, beauty, and bounty, as well as the means by which they can be obtained, only He sends them at the appropriate time.

Since He alone determines, apportions, creates, and spreads all our provisions before us as "heavenly tables," He alone deserves our gratitude and thanks. Attributing our attainment of His bounties to our own or to another's means or causes, in effect thereby proclaiming that He is not the true Owner, Creator, and Giver of all bounty, is like giving a huge tip to the servant who lays before us a magnificent feast and ignoring the host who is responsible for having it prepared and sent to us. Such an attitude reflects sheer ignorance and ingratitude, as mentioned in: *They know only the outward face of the life of the world (apparent to them), and they are completely unaware of (its face looking to) the Hereafter* (30:7).

True thankfulness in one's heart is manifested through the conviction and acknowledgment that all bounties are from God, and then ordering one's life accordingly. One can thank God verbally and through one's daily life only if one is personally convinced, and willingly acknowledges that his or her existence, life, body, physical appearance, and all abilities and accomplishments are from God only, as are all bounties obtained and consumed. This is stated in: *Do you not see that God has made serviceable unto you whatsoever is in the skies and whatsoever is in the earth, and has loaded you with His bounties seen or unseen?* (31:20), and: *He gives you of all that you ask Him; and if you reckon the bounties of God, you can never count them* (14:34).

Physical thankfulness is possible by using one's body, faculties, and abilities for the purposes for which they were created, and in performing the duties of servanthood that fall to one. On the other hand, some have stated that verbal thankfulness means the daily recitation of portions of the Qur'an, prayers, supplications, and God's Names. Being sincere and being certain or convinced of the truth of the Islamic faith is thankfulness of the heart. Physical thankfulness, according to others, means observing all acts of worship. Since thankfulness relates directly to all aspects or branches of belief and worship, it is regarded as being half the faith. With respect to this inclusiveness, it is considered together with patience, meaning that according to some people, thankfulness and patience are considered as the two halves of religious life.

In His eternal Speech, God Almighty repeatedly commands thankfulness and, as in the phrases *so that you may give thanks* (2:52) and *God will reward the thankful* (3:144), presents it as the purpose of creation and of the religion being sent. In such verses as: *If you are thankful I will add more unto you. But if you show ingratitude My punishment is terrible indeed* (14:7), He has promised abundant reward to the thankful and threatened the ungrateful with a terrible punishment. One of His own Names is the All-Thanking, which shows us that the way to obtain all bounties or favors is through thankfulness, which He returns with abundant reward. He exalts Prophets Abraham and Noah, upon them be peace, saying: *(Abraham was) thankful for*

His bounties (16:121) and *Assuredly, he (Noah) was a grateful servant* (17:3).

Although thankfulness is a religious act of great importance and significant "capital," few people are truly thankful: *Few of My servants are thankful* (34:13). Very few people live in full awareness of the duty of thankfulness, saying: *Shall I not be a servant grateful (to my Lord)?*, and try their best to perform their duty of thankfulness and order their lives accordingly.

The glory of humanity, upon him be peace and blessings, whose feet became swollen because of his long supererogatory prayer vigils (*tahajjud*), was a matchless hero of thankfulness. On one occasion, he told his wife 'A'isha: *Shall I not be a servant grateful to God?*[113] He always thanked God and recommended thankfulness to his followers, and prayed to God every morning and evening, saying: *O God. Help me mention You, thank You, and worship You in the best way possible.*[114]

Thankfulness is the deep gratitude and devotion of one who, receiving His bounties or favors, directs these feelings toward the One Who bestows such blessing, and the subsequent turning to Him in love, appreciation, and acknowledgment. The above Prophetic saying expresses this most directly.

People are thankful for many things: the provisions, home, and family with which they have been favored; wealth and health; belief, knowledge of God, and the spiritual pleasures bestowed on them; and the consciousness with which God favored them so they could open themselves to the knowledge that they must be thankful. If those who are thankful for such a consciousness use

---

[113] The Prophet, upon him be peace and blessings, asked 'A'isha: *Shall I not be a servant grateful to God?* in reply to her question: *Since God has forgiven all your sins that you may have committed and may commit in the future, why do you tire yourself so much by observing long prayer vigils?* Al-Bukhari, "Tahajjud," 6; Muslim, "Munafiqun," 79-81; Al-Tirmidhi, "Salat," 187.

[114] Nasa'i, "Sahw," 60.

their helplessness and destitution as "capital" and thank Him continuously, they will be among the truly thankful. It is narrated from God's Messenger, upon him be peace and blessings, that

> Prophet David, upon him be peace, asked God Almighty: *O Lord. How can I be thankful to You, since thanking You is another favor that requires thankfulness?* The Almighty responded: *Just now you have done it.*

I think this is what is expressed in: *We have not been able to thank You as thanking You requires, O All-Thanked One.*

One can be thankful by recognizing and appreciating Divine favors, for feeling gratitude to the One Who bestows favors depends to a great extent on due recognition and appreciation of such favors. Belief and Islam (including the Qur'an) lead one to recognize and appreciate favors and thus turn to God in gratitude. One can be more aware of these favors, and that they are given to us by God out of His mercy for our helplessness and inability to meet our own needs, in the light of belief and Islamic practices. This awareness urges us to praise the One Who bestows upon us the favors and bounties that we consume. Awakening to the meaning of: *As for the favor of Your Lord, proclaim it* (93:11), we feel a deep need to be grateful and thankful.

Everyone is naturally inclined to praise the good and the one who does good to him or her. However, until this feeling is aroused there is no awareness of being favored by someone else, just as fish are not conscious of living in water. Furthermore, these favors may be attributed to the means and causes used to obtain them. If it is blindness and deafness not to see and appreciate the favors we continuously receive, then it must be an unforgivable deviation to attribute them to various blind, deaf, and unfeeling means and causes. The Prophetic statements: *One who is not thankful for little is not thankful for abundance,*[115] and: *One who does not thank people does not thank God,*[116]

---

[115] Ibn Hanbal, *Musnad*, 4:278, 375.
[116] "Abu Dawud," Adab, 11; Tirmidhi, "Birr," 35.

express blindness and deafness to favors and remind us of the importance of being thankful. Such verses as: *Mention Me so that I will mention you, and give thanks to Me and do not be ungrateful to Me* (2:152), and: *Worship Him and give Him thanks* (29:17) tell us that it is God Who truly deserves to be thanked, and also remind us of His absolute Unity.

Thankfulness can be divided into three categories. The first category consists of thankfulness for those things that everyone, regardless of religion or spiritual attainment, desires. The second category consists of thankfulness for those things that, although apparently disagreeable or displeasing, reveal their true nature to those who can see them as favors requiring gratitude.

The third category of thankfulness is made up of thankfulness given by those who are loved by God and view favors or bounties from the perspective of the One Who bestows them. They spend their lives in spiritual pleasure that begins in the observation of God's manifestation of Himself through His favors, and take the greatest pleasure in worshipping Him. Although they are always enraptured with spiritual delight that flows from their love of Him, they are extremely careful of their relationship with Him.[117] Such people constantly strive to preserve the Divine blessings that have been bestowed upon them, and always search for what they have missed. While they constantly deepen their belief, love, and gratitude along the way toward Him, the "nets of their sight" are filled with different blessings and gifts.[118]

> *O God! Include us among Your servants whom You love, have made sincere, and have brought unto You. Grant peace and blessings to our Master, the Master of those loved, made sincere, and brought near unto You.*

---

[117] They do nothing that contradicts their being favored with those pleasures because of their nearness to Him. They are careful and self-possessed so that those delights do not lead them to do anything incompatible with self-possession.

[118] That is, their faculty of sight is satisfied by continuously seeing the manifestations of His Beauty and Grace.

Sabr (Patience)

Sabr literally means enduring, bearing, and resisting pain, suffering and difficulty, and being able to deal calmly with problems. In more general terms it means patience, which is one of the most important actions of the heart mentioned in the Qur'an. Because of its importance, patience is regarded as half of one's religious life (the other half is thankfulness).

The Qur'an orders patience in many verses, such as: *Seek help in patience and prayer* (2:45) and: *Endure, vie with each other in endurance* (3:199), and prohibits haste in verses like: *Show not haste concerning them (the unbelievers)* (46:35) and: *When you meet in battle those who do not believe, turn not your backs to them* (8:15). In many Qur'anic verses, God praises the patient ones, declares that He loves them, or mentions the ranks He has bestowed on them: *The patient and steadfast, and the truthful and loyal* (3:16); *God loves the patient ones* (3:145); and *Surely God is with the patient ones* (2:153).

The Qur'an mentions many other aspects of patience. For example: *If you endure patiently, this is indeed better for those who are patient* (16:126) advises patience as a preferable way in dealing with unbelievers while communicating God's Message to them. *We will certainly bestow on those who are patient their reward according to the best of what they used to do* (16:96) consoles patient people with the best of rewards to be given in the Hereafter. *If you have patience and guard yourselves against evil and disobedience, God will send to your aid five thousand angels with distinguishing marks, if they [your enemies] suddenly attack you* (3:124) promises the believers Divine aid in return for patience.

How meaningful is the following saying of the master of humanity concerning patience and thankfulness:

How remarkable a believer's affair is, for it is always to his advantage, and such a condition is only for a believer. If something good
happens to him he thanks God, which is to his advantage; if something bad happens to him he endures it, which is also to his advantage.[119]

The characteristics of patience can be grouped into five categories: enduring the difficulties associated with being a true servant of God or steadfastness in performing regular acts of worship; resisting the temptations of the carnal self and Satan to
commit sins; enduring heavenly or earthly calamities, which
includes resignation to Divine decrees; being steadfast in following the right path and not allowing worldly attractions to
cause deviation; and showing no haste in realizing hopes or plans
that require a certain length of time to achieve.

With respect to its degrees, patience can be divided into six
categories: showing patience for the sake of God; showing patience and attributing it to God (being convinced that God enables one to show patience); enduring patiently whatever comes
from God, knowing that He acts from His Wisdom; being resigned to whatever happens in the way of God; showing patience by not disclosing the mysteries of one's achieved spiritual
station and to preserve one's nearness to God; and resolving to
fulfill one's mission of communicating God's Message to people, despite one's deepest desire to die and meet with God.

There are other definitions of patience as well. For example,
preserving one's manners in the face of misfortune; being
steadfast when confronted with events and showing no sign of
being deterred; never giving in to one's carnal desires and the
impulses of one's temperament; accepting the commandments of
the Qur'an and the Sunna as a sort of invitation to Paradise; and
sacrificing all possessions, including one's soul and beloved
ones, for the sake of the True, Beloved One.

Those Qur'anic interpreters who were interested in the text's
secret or esoteric meanings have made the following commen-

---

[119] Muslim, "Zuhd," 64.

taries on the verse: *Endure, vie with each other in endurance, and continue your relation with God* (3:199):

> Be steadfast in performing your religious duties, endure whatever displeasing events happen to you, and maintain your love for God and desire to meet with Him. Or, be steadfast in fulfilling all your responsibilities for the sake of God and to please Him, and endure the difficulty of always being aware of His constant supervision over you and feeling His omnipresence. Or, be steadfast in following the Straight Path without any deviation, even when Divine bounties pour out onto you. Resolve to endure all difficulties and hardships, and maintain your connection or adherence to God whatever happens to you.

Another approach to patience is to attribute to God Almighty whatever is in the universe and happens therein and, while giving thanks for what appears pleasing, being resigned to what appears displeasing. When a believer unburdens himself or herself to God while trying to overcome a misfortune or hardship, a responsibility that is very hard to fulfill, or sins that he or she may have committed, this is not considered as a complaint against God. Rather, it is a believer's way of asking Him for help and seeking refuge in Him. In no way can such an action be considered a complaint or a protest against God or Divine Destiny. In reality, and according to one's intention, such an act may even be regarded as a supplication and an entreaty, as putting one's trust in Him or as submitting to Him.

The cry of Prophet Job to God: *Truly distress (disease, tribulation) has seized me. But You are the Most Compassionate of the Compassionate* (21:83) and the groaning of Prophet Jacob: *I only complain of my anguish and my sorrow unto God* (12:86) are supplications or entreaties for God's pity and compassion. God Almighty praised Job for being an excellent servant distinguished with patience and supplications: *We found him patient; how excellent a servant! Truly he was ever turning (to God) with supplications* (38:44).

One of the most distinguishing characteristics of Prophets and saints is their embodiment of patience in all of its manifold forms and degrees, and that without deviating from their utmost devotion to God, they do their best to communicate God's Message to people and bear all misfortune and difficulty arising therefrom. The glory of humanity, upon him be peace and blessings, who is a mercy for the whole of creation, declared: *Among mankind, those who are stricken with the most terrible of misfortunes are the Prophets, and then follow others according to their degree of faith.*[120]

Patience is an essential characteristic of those believers who are the most advanced in belief, spirituality, nearness to God, and who guide others to the truth. It is, moreover, the source of power for those advancing toward this final point. Since the most advanced people experience the most misfortune, they are perfect embodiments of patience, which is the price they pay for the rank bestowed on them. Others who have been destined to advance to that final point cross the distances traveled by others through different and frequent acts of worship, by enduring whatever happens to them. Of these, God's Messenger, upon him be peace and blessings, says:

> If God Almighty has destined one of His servants a rank or position which he cannot reach through his religious actions, He causes him to suffer from his own self and family, and equips him with patience to endure all his sufferings. He elevates him through patience to the rank destined.[121]

Thus the suffering to be endured, the difficulty in fulfilling one's responsibilities, and the pressure of sin contain potential mercy, mercy that is attained by one's patience. One subjected to such affliction should not unburden himself or herself to anybody else. How beautifully Fuduli says:

> You say you are a lover, then do not complain of the affliction of love;
>   By complaining, do not make others informed of your affliction.

---

[120] Al-Tirmidhi, "Zuhd," 56; Ibn Maja, "Fitan," 23; 'Abd Allah ibn 'Abd al-Rahman al-Darimi, "Riqaq," in *Sunan*, 2 vols. (Beirut: Dar al-Kitab al-'Arabi, 1987), 67.

[121] Abu Hatim Ibn Hibban, *Sunan*, 4:248; Al-Muttaqi al-Hindi, *Kanz al 'Ummal*, vol. 3, hadith no. 6822.

Travelers on the path to God should know how to burn and boil with love or be consumed with affliction, but never complain to others of such love and affliction. Even if crushed by difficulty or responsibility that is as heavy as mountains, they should not complain to others.

Rumi summarizes such a degree of patience as follows:

> In order to be sustenance for man, a source of strength for his knees, a "light" for his eyes, and a substance for the maintenance of his life, a grain of wheat must be buried in the bosom of the earth, germinate under it, and grow to emerge into the air. It must come into the air after a fierce struggle with the earth, and then be sown and threshed, and ground in a mill. After that, it must be kneaded, baked in an oven, and, finally, chewed by teeth, sent into the stomach, and digested.

To attain true humanity, each individual must be "sieved" or "distilled" many times to discover his or her true essence. Otherwise, the ability to develop one's potential to its fullest, to be truly human, is not possible:

> It is expected of God's servant to suffer,
> And of an aloe wood to burn.

Patience is an essential and most important dimension of servanthood to God, and is crowned with resignation, the highest spiritual rank in the sight of God, to whatever God has destined. •

Rida (Resignation)

Rida (resignation) means showing no rancor or rebellion against misfortune, and accepting all manifestations of Destiny without complaint and even peacefully. In other words, one should welcome all things and events, even those normally associated with distress and terror. Another succint definition of resignation is being satisfied with God's treatment whether it seems agreeable or not.

Even though believers must adopt resignation of their free will at the beginning of the spiritual journey, in reality it is a direct gift of God to those whom He loves. For this reason, unlike patience, neither God Almighty nor the Prophet, upon him be peace and blessings, commanded it; they only recommended it. Although there is a narration attributed to the Prophet—*Let him who does not endure misfortunes and show resignation to Divine decrees find another Lord for himself* [122]—the scholars of Traditions did not accept this as an authentic Prophetic Tradition. [123]

Some saints have considered resignation a higher station than reliance and surrender, while others have regarded it, like other states, as a Divine gift or radiance that sometimes appears and then disappears. Still others, like Imam Qushayri, have seen it as connected with or dependent upon the servant's free will in the beginning, and as a state or condition of the heart in the end. The Tradition: *One who is pleased with God as the Lord and*

---

[122] Al-Muttaqi al-Hindi, *Kanz al-'Ummal*, vol. 1, hadith no. 482.

[123] The writer says that resignation is not attained through one's efforts. Since it is a direct gift of the Almighty, a believer is not (absolutely) obliged to attain it. The author mentions it in order to answer possible objections to his view as based on this tradition. It is defective in its chain of transmission according to the rules of *hadith*.

Islam as the religion and Muhammad as the Prophet has tasted the delight of belief[124] suggests that a person must exercise his or her free will to obtain resignation in the beginning, although it is a Divine gift in the end.

Being pleased with God's Divinity means loving and paying due respect to Him, turning to Him in worship and for help, and expecting things only from Him. Being pleased with His Lordship signifies that we welcome His decrees for us, raise no objection to any misfortune befalling us (no matter how severe), confide in Him only concerning His treatment of us, and are pleased with whatever He does. Being pleased with the Prophet, upon him be peace and blessings, denotes unconditional surrender to him, preferring his guidance and directions over our personal views, and using all of our faculties to understand—not to criticize—his actions and words and the Revelations he transmitted. As for being pleased with Islam, as declared in: *He who seeks a religion other than Islam, it will not be accepted from him* (3:85) it is required that one accepts Islam as the ideal set of maxims and norms, and practices them in one's individual, familial, and social life.

In some circumstances, such a degree of resignation may cause one to feel or be left alone even when in a community. However, those who have acquired God's nearness and follow the way of the Prophet, upon him be peace and blessings, do not feel such estrangement, and those who have a deep familiarity with God do not feel lonely. Rather, they feel God as being nearer to themselves and overflow with greater love of and familiarity with Him when they are alone and pray to Him, saying: *O God, cause me to remain alone more frequently and do not leave me to the injustice of things that cause me to fall distant from You. Make me feel Your ever-present company.*

As mentioned earlier, resignation is a Divine gift that can be acquired only by an individual's conscious decision to exercise free will at the beginning of the journey. One can attain the rank

---

[124] Muslim, "Iman," 56; Ibn Hanbal, *Musnad*, 1:208.

of resignation through depth of belief, solemnity in religious actions, and such a profound consciousness of worshipping God that it is as if one were seeing Him. To be favored with the rank of resignation, one also must transcend the ranks of reliance, surrender, and commitment. Since it is extremely difficult to attain the rank of resignation by free will, God Almighty has not required it; He has only advised it and highly praised those who have attained it.

If one sets out on the journey to attain the rank of resignation at the end, he or she must be solemn in his or her relations with the Lord, gratefully accept all bestowed (and unsought) Divine gifts as His blessings, remain silent about any deprivation, fulfill all religious obligations even in times of distress, loneliness, and hardship, and pray in the presence of God Almighty with pleasure. The most essential foundation of resignation is a continuous feeling of His company in one's consciousness and experience, discovering Him afresh at every moment in one's heart.

Fear and hope relate to one's worldly life, for they render impossible all feelings of despair and security against God's punishment while in this world. They have no relevance to the Hereafter, except for the reward they cause to be bestowed in the Hereafter. By contrast, being pleased with God and loving Him continue eternally, and resignation to His judgment and being pleased with Him is a source of spiritual peace and happiness in both worlds.

This does not mean that those who have obtained resignation and God's pleasure or approval are free of anxiety, hardship, and suffering, for there remain many annoying and displeasing things on their way. However, champions of resignation regard such events as pure mercies, for resignation or God's pleasure changes the "poison" they drink into "elixir," and the troubles they encounter cause them to fall even deeper in love with the Beloved.

The way of resignation, although difficult to follow, is safe and direct. It sometimes leads the wayfarer to the summit of human perfection after a single attempt. Just as a believer can reach that summit by strenuous effort in the way of God or by studying the universe (as if it were a book) in order to feel and find God everywhere (although He is contained in neither time nor place), the summit can also be reached through one's inner suffering and sorrow arising from personal shortcomings and helplessness upon encountering difficulties while searching for a way to progress on the path.

Resignation results in a thrilling joy or a heavenly breeze caused by God's pleasure with the believer, a breeze that is proportional to the depth of one's fear and hope. It does not come from feeling God's nearness, worship and devotion, or from the struggle against sin and the temptations of one's carnal self and Satan. Rather, it is a spiritual delight merged with hope and expectation, regulated by self-possession, a direct gift from Him, and a breath of mercy associated only with this station of being pleased with God.

This station requires the self-regulation of one's thoughts, considerations, plans, hopes, expectations, feelings, and actions according to God's Will. Thus, seeing resignation as a way to experience pleasure and to delight in the expectation of acquiring that pleasure shows one's disrespect of this station, which is based on the purity of one's intention and sincerity. In reality, this applies to all other states and stations attained through actions of the heart, or which are themselves actions of the heart. One must love and pursue His approval or pleasure for His sake only.

Heroes of the spiritual life have expressed their views about resignation and being pleased with God since the early days of Sufism. According to Dhu al-Nun al-Misri, resignation means preferring God's wishes over one's own in advance, accepting His decree without complaint, based on the realization that whatever God wills and does is good,[125] and overflowing with

---

[125] Al-Qushayri, *Al-Risala*, 195.

love of Him even while in the grip of misfortune. 'Ali Zayn al-'Abidin describes resignation as an initiate's determination not to pursue anything opposed to God's Will and pleasure.[126] According to Abu 'Uthman, resignation denotes welcoming with the same mood all Divine decrees and acts, regardless of whether they issue from His Grace or His Majesty or Wrath, and having no conscious preference for one or the other. God's Messenger referred to this when he said: *I ask You for resignation after You have decreed something.*[127] Being pleased in advance with God's decree means being determined to show resignation, while resignation signifies enduring calamity when it occurs.

In short, resignation means that an initiate feels no resentment against or displeasure with whatever issues from God's Divinity or Lordship. Rather, the initiate welcomes it gladly and is ready to accept or endure his or her fate without complaint. The initiate does not upset the balance of his or her heart. Rather, he or she preserves personal integrity and straightforwardness even when confronted with the most distressing and shocking events, considers God's predestination as recorded in the Supreme Preserved Tablet, and thus feels no regret or sorrow for what happens.

For ordinary people, resignation means not objecting to what God has willed for them. For those with a deeper spiritual knowledge of God, resignation means welcoming their individual destinies. For those who live a life of profound spirituality, resignation means that, without paying attention to their own considerations, they are always attentive to what He wants them to do and how He wants them to be. The verses: *O soul at rest, return to your Lord, well pleasing and pleased. Enter among My servants, and enter My Paradise* (89:27-30) encompass all degrees of resignation, and contain responses to the desires of those resigned to the Divine Will and Destiny.

---

[126] Ibid., 195.

[127] Al-Nasa'i, "Sahw," 62; Ibn Hanbal, *Musnad,* 5:191.

As seen in these same verses, attaining the station of resignation and pleasing God and being pleased with Him depend upon one's turning to God Almighty. This means complete devotion to, reliance upon, and surrender to Him and committing all affairs to Him. One who has attained this station longs for death and meeting with God, dies with their heart at rest, and is included among the righteous in Paradise.

From another perspective, ordinary people show their resignation by ordering their lives according to God's commandments in willing submission to His Lordship and administrative authority. This is expressed in the verses: *Say: Shall I seek another than God for Lord, when He is Lord of all things?* (6:165), and: *Say: Shall I choose for a protecting friend other than God, the Originator of the heavens and the earth, Who feeds and Himself is not fed?* (6:14) Such a degree of resignation is essential to whoever aspires to true belief in God's Unity and true love of God. Every believer must consciously submit himself or herself to God's guidance; associate no partners with Him in belief and in ordering one's life; love Him alone as the Lord, Deity, and Ruler of humanity and the universe; and love others who are worthy to be loved only in His name and in accordance with the limits He has established.

The second degree of resignation, that of those with a certain degree of knowledge of God, is manifested in their welcoming God's decrees and ordinances without objection. It is also seen in the control they have acquired over their hearts, a control so strong that their hearts do not swerve, even for one moment. Such resignation is regarded as the connection between God and those hearts furnished with knowledge of Him.

The third degree of resignation is attained by those purified, saintly scholars who are pleased with what pleases God. One who has been rewarded with such resignation feels no personal anger, joy, or grief. Such a person, no longer feeling, thinking, or desiring for himself or herself, experiences the pleasure of annihilation in the Lord, for only His Will and decisions remain.

The first degree of resignation, obligatory upon every believer, is the beginning of the way that leads to nearness to God, for it is related to free will and is a requirement of belief in His Unity. The second degree must be acquired, both because it is the continuation of the first and the basis of the third degree, and because it leads one to consider nearness to God.

The third degree, a Divine gift rather than a station attainable by free will and individual effort, is neither obligatory nor necessary. However, it is commendable to desire it wholeheartedly. This degree encompasses the first two, for aspiring after complete resignation and living so as to attain it is an essential principle of Islamic life. However, its full attainment is a gift bestowed in return for this aspiration. In other words, the first two degrees relate to God's Names and Attributes, which can be attained by journeying in their shadow or their guidance, while the third is connected with the reward, enlightenment, or radiance given in return for them.

The verse: *Their reward is with their Lord; Gardens of Eden, beneath which rivers flow; where they will dwell forever. God is well pleased with them and they are well pleased with Him. That is for him who fears his Lord reverently* (98:8) points to all of these degrees. This same truth was expressed by our master, upon him be peace and blessings, who said: *One who is well pleased with God as the Lord, with Islam as the religion, and with Muhammad (pbuh) as the Messenger has tasted the pleasure of faith.*

I hope that the following considerations will direct the feelings and thoughts of those who desire to attain resignation, help them to overcome the difficulties encountered on this path, and to control and resist their worldly and carnal impulses.

· Human beings are only role players in the Divine drama played out on the stage of this world. Therefore, they have no right or authority to interfere with the quality or form of their assigned part. Whatever happens to an individual has been predetermined by God, Who considered his or her free will, actions, and thoughts in this world. Only God can change this.*

· If one really loves God, whatever comes from Him must be welcomed. It is very difficult to perceive the wisdom and good or purpose in some events. Sometimes what is good for us is hidden in distressing events: *It may be that you dislike a thing although it is good for you, and love a thing although it is bad for you. God knows, but you know not* (2:216).

· A Muslim is one who has fully submitted to God. Thus, such an individual cannot be displeased with God's actions and operations. A believer has a good opinion of everybody else, so how can he or she be suspicious of God? The Qur'an forbids us to suspect other people (48:12); how much worse it would be if we suspected God and His acts! Since all things and events were preordained and created by God, and since whatever He creates is either good in itself or on account of its result, a Muslim should keep his or her heart at rest and always be optimistic.

· If our obligations or responsibilities, as well as the misfortunes and difficulties we endure or seek to overcome, have an essential place in our training and education to prepare us for the eternal life of happiness in the Hereafter, then we should fulfill them or endure them willingly. An individual's resignation to or being pleased with whatever comes from Him means that He is also pleased with that particular individual. Being displeased with the acts and manifestations of Divine Lordship causes distress, grief, and restlessness, while living resigned to God's decrees

---

* **Translator's Note:** God's "predetermination," which we call Destiny, is almost identical with His Knowledge. As God is not confined by time, He can see one's past, present, and future at the same time. He therefore "knows" what one will do "before" he or she does it. God's knowing beforehand how someone will act does not compel the person to act that way; rather, it shows that one's free will is included in what God has "predetermined" for him or her.

gives relief and exhilaration, even though one has to suffer
great difficulties. In short, the continuous pursuit of resignation is an invitation to Divine succor.

· Resignation to Destiny and the manifestations of God, the
Truth, is a very important means of obtaining happiness.
The truthful and confirmed one, upon him be peace and
blessings, illuminates this: *It is fortunate for man to show
resignation to what God decrees, while it is unfortunate for
him to feel indignation against what God decrees.*[128] Being
resigned to God's decrees and disposals fills one's heart
with breezes from the Divine Realm, while displeasure
with them fills it with whims and suspicions coming from
Satan. Those who resign themselves to His decrees make
their lives into an "embroidery" of golden threads of
thankfulness, while those who are displeased with them
grind even their most positive works into nothing between
the millstones of ingratitude. Showing such displeasure, an
all-too-common attitude on the part of many, is one of
Satan's most effective ways of invading one's soul.

· A believer may join the inhabitants of the heavens by welcoming God's treatment, which is an honor bestowed by
God. One who is pleased with God is following the right
guidance, while one who is not pleased follows nothing
more than personal fancies. Resignation to God's judgments or decrees means preferring His wishes to our own.
It hardly needs saying what the opposite attitude implies.

· Resignation is like an orchard whose trees yield the fruits
of worship and devotion; sins and offenses are the results
of being deprived of it. Resignation prevents personal
conflicts with God in the believer's inner world, and
means respecting the principle expressed in the supplication of the Prophet, upon him be peace and blessings: *It
is pure justice in whatever way You judge me.* The first sin

---

[128] Al-Tirmidhi, "Qadar," 15; Ibn Hanbal, *Musnad*, 1:168.

was committed when Satan did not resign himself to what
God had decreed for him.[129]

· One can have no greater reward or higher rank than God's
being pleased with him or her, which is only attainable by
personal resignation to what He has decreed. This is also
the greatest reward that one can receive in Paradise: *God
has promised the believers, men and women, Gardens
beneath which rivers flow, to dwell therein forever, and
beautiful mansions in Gardens of Eden. But God's good
pleasure [His being pleased with them] is greater still.
That is the supreme triumph* (9:72).

· Resignation is based on the most important essential of
religion: reliance upon God. Its essential quality can be
perceived by means of certainty about God's existence and
Unity. It is embedded in love of God, and causes one to
gain eternal happiness. It is rooted in loyalty to God and
truthfulness, and denotes actual thankfulness. Resignation
is such a magical vehicle that those who obtain it will
reach their destination quickly. Love and sincerity, as well
as penitence and contrition, are flowers growing in the
climate of resignation. It is useless to search for such
virtues or qualities in hearts that are not set on resignation
and obtaining God's pleasure.

· However numerous those rewards given in return for
acting and speaking to attain God's pleasure may be, they
can be counted and are therefore limited. The rewards
given for such actions as resignation, which is done with
the heart, are proportional to the heart's depth and so
cannot be estimated.

As the greatest rank in God's sight, resignation or God's
pleasure is a final target that has been sought by the greatest
members of humanity, from the glory of creation, upon him be

---

[129] Ibn Hanbal, *Musnad*, 1:391, 452.

peace and blessings, to all the other Prophets, saints, and purified scholars who have passed the final test through sincerity, certainty, reliance, surrender, and confidence. They have surmounted many difficulties and obstacles, and bore many unendurable sufferings and torments. The following verses seek to describe the sighs of such people:

> The suffering You cause is more pleasing than having fortune,
> And Your vengeance is lovelier to me than my own soul.
> I am in love with both His torment and His favor;
> How strange it is that I am in love with things opposite to each other.
> By God, if I go from this thorn of affliction to the garden of delight,
> I will be one who, like a nightingale, always groans or sighs.
> How strange it is that when a nightingale starts to sing,
> It sings melodies of both the thorn and the rose.

The following verse of Nasimi is also beautiful:

> I am a suffering lover, O dear One, I will not abandon You;
> Even if You cut through my chest with a dagger, I will not abandon You.
> Even if they cut me into two from head to foot like Zachariah,
> Put your saw on my head, O Carpenter, I will not abandon You.
> Even if they burn me into cinders and blow away my ashes,
> They will hear my ashes sigh: *O Veiler (of sins), I will not abandon You.*

The rank or station of resignation, of being pleased with God and obtaining His pleasure, includes all other ranks. The melodies sung in it are: *Whatever You do to me or however You treat me, it is good.*

O God! Guide us to what You will love and be pleased with, and bestow peace and blessings upon our Master and the Master of the Messengers.

Inbisat (Expansion)

Literally meaning growing larger and deeper, spreading and expanding, Sufis use *inbisat* to signify the relaxing of one's heart, to the extent allowed by the Shari'a, so that it can embrace everybody and please them with one's gentle words and pleasant manners. In the context of one's relationship with God Almighty, it denotes a spiritual state that combines fear and hope. Those who have attained this state are awed by being in the Presence of God, and feel exhilarated by the breezes of delight and joy blowing in His Presence. They are awed while inhaling, and feel delight when exhaling.

As pointed out in the brief description above, expansion can be dealt with in two categories: our relationship with the created, and our relationship with the Creator.

With respect to our relationship with the created, expansion means that we are careful of our connection with God and the Truth; that we live in our community as one of its inhabitants, being open with and showing respect to everyone; and that we treat people according to their level of understanding.

The noble Prophet, upon him be peace and blessings, was sincere and frank with those around him, and avoided ceremony or formality. He spoke according to his listeners' level of understanding, and sometimes made wise and meaningful jokes. Although he suffered inwardly from the unbelief, injustice, and sins he witnessed, and was anxious about everyone's position in the afterlife, he always smiled and behaved pleasantly. As said in the *Minhaj*: *A heart is like a mirror: too much and too frequent solemnity may cause it to steam up, and the only way to remove that steam is to tell pleasant jokes.*

With respect to our relationship with God Almighty, expansion signifies the simultaneous experiencing of fear and hope in our souls. Being states of the soul, fear and hope are usually found in those who have just started to advance on the path to God. Expansion, on the other hand, is a state of those with knowledge of God and, moreover, is a dimension of the heart's liveliness. The state resembling the expansion of those still striving to reach this level is an exhilaration coming from knowledge of God. This may lead them to relax in their relationship with God, and thus lose their self-control and self-possession.

Expansion appears when a traveler on the path of God is completely freed from carnal desire and passion, and becomes a bright "mirror" to reflect God's Names and Attributes. This station, whether called the Station of Combination (where the traveler experiences God's Existence and Unity) or Annihilation (where the traveler feels utterly annihilated in the throes of ecstatic love of God and the perception of God's Existence and Unity, and wholly forgets himself or herself), is a mysterious point where the traveler directs himself or herself according to the Divine inspirations received and assumes "colors" unknown to everybody else. It is impossible for such people to conceal their expansion, while it is insolent of those who have not attained it to talk about it. How aptly Rumi expresses this situation:

> If the king's courtier behaves in an affected manner to attract the king's attention, you must not attempt to do so, for you do not have the document (to justify your doing so). O one who cannot be freed from the restrictions of this transient life, how can you know what (the stations of) annihilation, drunkenness, and expansion mean?

Indeed, servants of the body cannot be aware of the states of the spirit. It is impossible for those imprisoned in the body to be aware of spirituality. We should ask those souls who have been burnt and "roasted" many times in the fire God's love about the pains of a heart that has been cleft open, and their expansion and contraction.

Qast and 'Azm (Decision and Resolution)

Qast means confidence, determination, choosing, and single-mindedness, thinking and reasoning moderately and deliberately, and living a moderate and balanced life. For Sufis, this term represents an initiate's pursuit of love and the pleasure of God, the Truly Beloved One, and the intent to realize this goal:

> The heart is the home of God, clean it of others than Him,
> So that the All-Merciful may descend into His home at night.

The couplet above, recorded by Ibrahim Haqqi of Erzurum in his *Ma'rifetname* (Book of Knowledge), expresses the intention to obtain true love and God's pleasure, and tells how this can be realized. It concisely describes how decision becomes resolution and resolution destination. The only way to obtain peace of mind and be at rest without going to extremes and being exposed to spiritual problems and pain is to seek the love and pleasure of God, and to order one's life around this aim. Rumi says:

> A heart devoid of the Friend and seeking Him cannot be freed from trouble and pain. As for a head in which there is no love of the Friend, do not attempt to find any meaning and value in it, for it consists of bones and skin.

Those who have set their hearts on Him and have decided to reach Him never ignore any way that leads to Him nor do they neglect to meet the necessities of traveling on the way.[130] Even if they turn their eyes from Him for a single moment to look to

---

[130] There is more than one way to God. It is said that there are as many ways or paths to God as the number of breaths taken by people. Such a statement is said to express the differences in people's temperaments and moods. In addition, spiritual orders use different rituals to help their initiates make progress on the spiritual path.

others, they sigh for a whole lifetime. How unfortunate is the one who lives unaware of a way leading to Him. What a great loss, impossible to compensate, it is to fall and get stuck on the way after embarking on it.

Decision first appears and develops in the heart, grows firmer and stronger as a feeling, and then becomes a very powerful drive directing one toward his or her destination. In this context, decision signifies an intention and resembles a seed sown in the heart's soil. If the one who has this intention or seed in his or her heart receives help from God Almighty, the seed germinates and grows into an elaborate, fruitful tree. After a few steps taken in decision, one finds resolution. Resolution can be defined as a determination to do something, as being steadfast in one's pursuit, and consciously fulfilling all responsibilities undertaken. Resolution is the first step toward the "heavens" of reliance and surrender. The Qur'an describes this step and the final point to be reached: *When you are resolved, rely on (or put your trust in) God* (3:159). If this first step can be taken through reliance on and submission to God, then the road becomes level and easy to walk on, and one travels it as if flying through the air.

Decision and resolution are two important dimensions or functions of willpower. Every traveler who intends to make a long journey must stop at the station of decision and resolution to receive the permit or visa, given by God, in order to progress to higher stations. Only after this does the journey truly begin. One who has taken the wings of decision and resolution feels attracted toward the goal and, no longer advancing by his or her own power, is taken to it. A friend of God says: *Whoever overflows with the desire to meet with God, despite his inability to fulfill the requirements of the way leading to his goal, God Himself comes to him*. God then becomes his or her eyes with which to see, ears with which to hear, and tongue with which to speak.

For the traveler who flies along on the wings of decision and resolution, meeting with God means finding subsistence in or through annihilation. For those whom God wills and desires to meet with, it means subsistence within subsistence,[131] and they suffer no trouble or pain in the "virtuous circle"[132] where they encounter good after good. In this circle pain changes into pleasure, and wrath or chastisement are manifested as favors. One who has reached this point always utters in pleasure: *Whatever comes from You, whether it be a favor or punishment, is good.* With a cup of resignation in one's hand, he or she sips whatever comes from God, the Truth, as if it were the water of Paradise.

"Can you Drink
the cup"
by Henri Nouwen

---

[131] This phrase denotes the concept of compound subsistence, defined as a "firmer subsistence" and as "being well-versed or grounded in subsistence."

[132] This is the opposite of the "vicious circle" that so many people encounter in their daily lives.

Irada, Murid, and *Murad* (Will, the Willing One, and the Willed One)

Irada (will) is both a verb and a noun. As a verb, it means to choose between two things, to desire. As a noun, it means the mental power by which a person can direct his or her thoughts and actions. Will has been defined by those living a spiritual life as overcoming carnal desires, resisting animal appetites, and always preferring, in complete submission to His Will, God's wish and pleasure over one's own. A willing disciple (*murid*) never relies on his or her own power, and is absolutely submitted to the Will of the All-Powerful, Who holds all of creation in His Grasp. As for the one willed (*murad*), he or she overflows with love of God and never considers or aspires to anything other than obtaining His pleasure. Such a person has become a favorite of God.

According to the verse: *They desire only to gain His favor* (6:52), will is the first station on the path to God and the first harbor from which one sets sail for eternity.[133] Almost everyone who sets sail for the infinite first comes to this harbor, from where an impetus to reach the ultimate destination is gained. Journeying toward this destination is proportional to the traveler's purity of intention, the degree and quality of his or her relationship with the world and material things, and the power of the driving force derived from this harbor and from the inner desire to undertake this voyage. In proportion to the help of God

---

[133] Eternity, in addition to meaning eternal life in the Hereafter, is also used to describe the expansion of feelings, emotions, and reflections that one feels inwardly. An individual has infinite, eternal desires and ambitions, and he or she can experience in his or her heart the (eternal) pleasures of Paradise and of being loved by God and loving Him.

and the strength of the disciple's willpower, some traverse the distance between the harbor and the destination at a walking pace, others at the speed of a spaceship or of light, and still others at a speed that cannot be measured. The Ascension of the Prophet, the spiral ascents of a saint, and the journeying of a dervish are good examples of what can be achieved by the will, the willing one, and the willed one when supported by the help of God, the Truth.

There is a derivative relation between will and the willing one (disciple). Just as material or natural causes are veils between superficial views and Divine Grandeur and Dignity, so that those who cannot understand the reality behind things and events should not blame God Almighty for what appears to be disagreeable, so too a person's willpower is only a shadow of the shadow of the Will of the One Who *does whatever He wills in whatever way He wills* (85:16). Just as a shadow is dependent on the substance, any will created is dependent on the Creator. Similarly, the liveliness and attraction observed in a mirror do not belong to the objects' reflections, but to the objects themselves. Nevertheless, it is difficult to understand this and distinguish between a shadow and the original.

Until the traveler perceives that one's personal will is a dim reflection of the Absolute Will (of the All-Willing One) and advances as far as, or rises as high as, the station of being the one willed or desired, one freed from the captivity of the body and thoughts to become a person of pure spirituality and conscience, he or she will always regard his or her will as having a separate, independent existence. Indeed, a traveler is willing at the beginning of the way and willed at the end of it; one is willing while exerting efforts to make servanthood second nature, and one is willed at the point where his or her relation with God is an indispensable dimension of his or her being; one is willing while searching the ways to be loved and desired, and is willed when seeing an imprint of Him on everything and weaving a lacework of spiritual pleasure with the threads of knowledge and love of God.

There are many stations between the beginning of certainty that comes from knowledge and the final point of certainty that comes from experience. Every station is both an end and a beginning; one road begins there, while another one terminates. For example, according to many: *Open and expand my breast for me* (20:25) is an end, while it is a beginning compared with: *Have We not expanded your breast for you?* (94:1). Also, for many: *My Lord! Show me Yourself, so that I may gaze upon You* (7:143) is a final station, while it is the beginning of the way extending to the station expressed in: *His sight swerved not, nor did it go wrong* (53:17). Again: *Assuredly, my Lord is with me. He will guide me* (26:62) means awareness of God's company, while it is not comparable with the exalted truth or reality mentioned in: *Do not be grieved, for God is with us* (9:40).

In the beginning, loyalty, faithfulness, and resolution are of fundamental importance, while solemnity, self-possession, and mannerliness are most important at the end of the journey. Those who have erred at the beginning cannot advance far, while those who have erred at the end are reproved.

One important source from which willpower is fed is the traveler's care and sensitivity in fulfilling his or her responsibilities and constant supplication to God. Moreover, dependant on the traveler's perseverance in supererogatory acts or duties of worship God Almighty may become his or her eyes with which to see, ears with which to hear, and hands with which to grasp.[134]

---

[134] Al-Bukhari, "Riqaq," 38; Ibn Hanbal, *Musnad*, 6:256.

Yaqin (Certainty)

Yaqin (certainty) means having no doubt about the truth of a matter and arriving at accurate, doubt-free knowledge through exact verification. Used also to mean verification, seeking certainty, examining, and exerting strenuous effort to arrive at certainty, certainty is a spiritual station that a traveler on the path has reached and experienced. It is obtained only by those who have an innate capability to progress and develop inwardly. This term is not used for God's Knowledge, which is infinite and therefore neither increases nor decreases. God does not have such a Name as "One having certainty or giving certainty." In addition, certainty is a degree reached through study and the verification of something previously doubted. The Divine Being neither doubts nor needs verification.

According to truth-seeking scholars, *yaqin* means certainty or conviction of the truth expressed in the essentials of faith, including primarily one's doubt-free belief in God's Existence and Unity. It is also defined as reaching that conviction through observing or experiencing the essence or truth of those essentials in which regular people believe, and discerning or penetrating the realms beyond this material one.

Certainty may also be regarded as a point, final in one respect and initial in another, reached by using all sources of knowledge and ways of observation and discernment. A traveler who has reached this point frequently sails for what is eternal, realizing ascension in his or her heart and reaching the horizon of: *His sight swerved not, nor did it go wrong* (53:17). He or she travels amidst Divine manifestations in the material and immaterial realms, and is favored with a tongue to speak, eyes to

see, and ears to hear the truths contained in the Supreme Sign.[135]
That is, repeated observation and study of the book of the universe, of the things and events contained in it, allows the traveler
to eternity to perceive the meanings of the inimitable signs special to God.[136]

By repeatedly observing and reflecting on the scenes presented for study in the outer world, as well as those in his or her
inner world, truths beyond the visible realm are unveiled to the
traveler. Also, by living in the brilliant, mysterious climate of Divine Revelation, namely the Qur'an and the Sunna, one feels the
manifestation of the Hidden Treasure in his or her heart. The
believer becomes aware of and experiences the tokens and signs
issuing from the prism of his or her conscience, which reflects
the rays of Divine gifts coming from the outer world, his or her
inner world, and the Divine Revelation, and sends them to his or
her senses and faculties. Certainty, in this meaning and degree,
is a gift with which God favors those near to Him.

Even in its least degree, certainty is so strong that it fills the
heart with light, removes the mist of doubt from the mind, and
causes breezes of joy, satisfaction, and exhilaration to blow in
one's inner world. As pointed out by Dhu al-Nun al-Misri,
certainty causes the heart to overflow with the desire to reach
eternity. This engenders the desire to live an austere life, for
asceticism allows one to think and speak with wisdom. One who
takes the wing of asceticism and flies to the realm of wisdom
never forgets what the end will be, always thinks of the afterlife,
and always feels God's company, even when with other people.[137]

In the early steps of certainty, the veil between the material
and immaterial sides of existence begins to be removed and, a

---

[135] "The Supreme Sign" is a Qur'anic expression that is generally held to be the
sign by which God is known most clearly.

[136] God's signs, the signs of His existence and Unity, are displayed by everything
in the language of wisdom, coherence, beneficence, and relation to other things.
It is like a seal designed by Him to prove His Unity.

[137] Al-Qushayri, *Al-Risala*, 180.

few steps further, the traveler discerns the realm beyond this material world. With his or her heart filled with Divine manifestations, which result in the attainment of peace and satisfaction, the believer is freed absolutely from all doubt about the truths of faith. Like 'Ali ibn Abi Talib, may God be pleased with him, some who have attained this degree of certainty have declared: *Even if the veil between the seen and the Unseen were to lift, my certainty would not increase.*[138] A few steps further on is the station where one journeys in the pure realm of Divine gifts, which eyes have never seen, ears have never heard, nor have minds ever conceived.

To gain certainty, an initiate beginning the journey must try to do what is necessary to reach certainty. However, one can only reach this station when God bestows it as a blessing and gift. Without acquiring due knowledge of God, one cannot reach certainty. Knowledge of God is acquired through a correct view of and perspective on objects and events; the ability to think in a correct and balanced manner; purity of intention; the study of the signs of God's Existence and Unity; and finally knowledge of God is required through reflection on His acts and the manifestations of His Names and Attributes. Knowledge of God is a light illuminating the initiate's inner and outer worlds, a light shining from all corners of existence. Under the rays of this light, the initiate sees everything as it really is and, being freed from the confines of multiplicity (of objects and events), discerns Divine Unity and is enraptured with indescribable spiritual pleasure.

Although an initiate may feel uneasy during the early stages on the way to certainty, he or she will be lost in inconceivable pleasure and peace at the end. Those who cannot distinguish between what is felt in the beginning and what is experienced at the end wrongly conclude that certainty is risky; however, those who constantly feel God's company and the resulting spiritual delight enjoy peace and security from all spiritual trouble and

---

[138] Al-Qari, *Asrar al-Marfu'a*, 286.

possible deviation. Uneasiness and trouble are felt only at the beginning. As for certainty being risky, all stations confront the traveler with some degree of risk. The Prophet, upon him be peace and blessings, declared: *Even I could not be saved (from Hellfire or God's punishment through my own actions), if God did not embrace me in His mercy.*[139] As for being secure from trouble and deviation and gaining peace, these are the fruits that God causes certainty to yield.

As referred to in some verses of the Qur'an, Sufis classify certainty in three categories:

· Certainty coming from knowledge: Having a strong, firm belief in or conviction of all the essentials of faith, primarily in God's Existence and Unity, acquired through correct observation and study of the relevant signs and evidence.

· Certainty coming from direct observation or seeing: Having an indescribable degree of certainty and knowledge of God acquired through unveiling and observing the immaterial truths invisible to ordinary believers and on which the essentials of belief are based.

· Certainty coming from direct experience: Being favored with God's constant company, without any veils and in a way that only the one receiving this favor can perceive. Some have interpreted this as self-annihilation in God and gaining subsistence by Him.

These three degrees of certainty can be summed up in the following examples: A person's knowledge of death (before he or she dies), acquired by observing or studying the body in a biological context, can be an example of certainty coming from knowledge. Witnessing some metaphysical phenomena, such as seeing the angel who has come to remove one's soul and catching glimpses of the intermediate world of the grave, may

---

[139] Al-Bukhari, "Riqaq," 18; Muslim, "Munafiqun," 71-8.

be regarded as a kind of certainty coming from direct observation. The certainty gained by actually experiencing death is a certainty coming from direct experience.

Certainty about abstract truths, such as the nature of God's Names and Attributes that arise from direct observation, for example, pertains to one's personal experience. It is therefore beyond my ability to explain this.

Dhikr (Recitation of God's Names)

Literally meaning mentioning, remembrance, and rec-
ollection, in the speech of the Sufis *dhikr* denotes regular
recitation of one or some of God's Names at one time. Some spiritual or Sufi orders prefer to recite: *Allah* (the proper Name of the
Divine Being); others recite: *There is no god but God*, the
declaration of Divine Unity; and others recite one or a few of the
other Names, according to the choice of the order's master.

Like thankfulness, such recitation is a duty of servanthood
to be performed both verbally and actively, and also with one's
heart and other conscience faculties. Verbal recitation ranges
from mentioning God Almighty with all His Beautiful Names
and sacred Attributes; praising, exalting, and glorifying Him;
proclaiming one's helplessness and destitution before Him in
prayer and supplication; reciting and following His Book (the
Qur'an); and announcing His signs in nature and the seal special
to Him on each object and event.

Recitation by the conscience faculties, primarily the heart,
consists of reflecting on the proofs of His Existence and Unity,
and His Names and Attributes that glow in the book of creation
(the universe), meditating on His orders and prohibitions, His
promises and threats, and the reward and punishment issuing
from His Lordship to design or order our lives, and trying to
penetrate the mysteries behind the veil of visible existence by
studying creation and following certain spiritual disciplines. In
addition, one can repeatedly observe the heavenly beauties
manifested as a result of such penetration; one comes to the
conclusion that whatever exists in the universe pulses with
messages from the high empyrean world, manifesting the
meaning of the invisible world and functioning as a window
upon the Truth of Truths.

Those who feel this constant pulsing existence, hear the invisible world speaking eloquently, and observe the manifestations of Grace and Majesty through those windows are so enraptured with such unimaginable spiritual pleasure that one hour spent with such pleasure is equal to hundreds of years spent without it. As a result, they advance along their way to eternity immersed in Divine gifts and spiritual delight. When the one reciting feels the light of His Glorified Face surrounding all existence, he or she is rewarded with the sight of indescribable scenes and, becoming aware of all the other beings reciting God's Names in the same tongue, begins to recite His Names.

Reciting God's Names sometimes causes the person reciting to enter a trance-like state in which their self is lost. Those who enter this entranced state or ecstatic contemplation utter such phrases as: *There is none existent save He, There is nothing seen save He*, and *There is no god but God*. There are others who, meaning and keeping in mind all Divine Names according to the inclusiveness of their consciousness, pronounce only *but God* and continue to declare His Unity. These seconds spent in this atmosphere of nearness to God and His company, the seconds of light and radiance, are much happier and more rewarding with respect to eternal life (in the Hereafter) than years spent with no light. This is what is referred to in a saying attributed to the Prophet, upon him be peace and blessings: *I have a time with my God when neither any angel nearest to God nor any Prophet sent as Messenger can compete with me.* [140]

Active or bodily recitation consists in practicing religion with utmost care, enthusiastically performing all obligations, and consciously refraining from all prohibitions. Verbal profundity and awareness largely depend on active recitation, which also means knocking on the door of Divinity, searching for admittance, proclaiming one's helplessness and destitution, and taking refuge in the Divine Power and Wealth.

---

[140] Al-'Ajluni, *Kashf al-Khafa'*, 2:173.

One who regularly and repeatedly mentions God, or recites one or some of His Names, is taken under His protection and supported by Him, as if having made a contract with Him. The verse: *Remember and mention Me, and I will remember and mention you* (2:152) expresses this degree of recitation, by which one's innate destitution becomes a source of wealth, and helplessness a source of power. This verse also means that one's regular remembrance and worship of God will result in His bestowal of favors and bounties.

Invoking and calling upon Him brings forth His favors. One who remembers Him even while going about his or her daily affairs and preoccupations will find all obstacles removed in both this world and the next. His company will always be felt, and He will befriend one left alone and in need of friends. If one remembers and mentions Him during times of ease and comfort, His Mercy will reach one during times of trouble and pain. Those who struggle in His way to spread His Name will be saved from humiliation in both this world and the Hereafter. Such sincere endeavors will be rewarded with special favors and ranks that one cannot now imagine.

The desire to mention Him and recite His Names will be rewarded with Divine help, so that such activities can continue and guidance can be increased. The continuation of the second part of the above verse (2:152), that is: *Give thanks to Me and do not show ingratitude to Me*, suggests a virtuous circle in which a believer passes from recitation to thankfulness, and from thankfulness to recitation.

Recitation is the essence of all types or acts of worship, and the origin of this essence is the Qur'an. Then come the luminous, celebrated words of the Prophet, to whom the Islamic Shari'a was sent. All recitation, whether audible or silent, attracts and embodies the manifestations of the light of God's Glorified "Face." It also is the proclamation of God to all human beings and jinn, and the spreading of His Name throughout the world in order to show one's thankfulness for His manifest and hidden favors. When there is almost no one left to proclaim His Name, existence will be meaningless. According to the Prophet, upon him be peace and blessings, the universe's total destruction will take place when there are almost no people left to proclaim His Name.[141]

Recitation, irrespective of its style, is the safest and soundest way leading to God. Without recitation, it is difficult to reach God. When the traveler remembers Him in his or her conscience and puts this remembrance into words with his or her tongue and other faculties, an inexhaustible source of support and (spiritual) provision is tapped.

Recitation signifies a journey toward Him. When one starts to mention Him or recites His Names both verbally and through feelings and actions, as well as in one's heart as a chorus, one enters a mysterious vehicle that ascends to the realm where spirits fly. Through the slightly opened doors of the heavens, indescribable scenes are beheld.

There is not a specific time for reciting God's Names. Although the five prescribed daily prayers, the chief act of worship, are performed at the five appointed times and cannot be performed at certain times (e.g., during sunrise and sunset, and when the Sun is at the zenith at noon), a believer can mention God and recite His Names whenever he or she wishes: *They mention God standing, sitting, and lying down* (3:190). There is no restriction of time or manner concerning the recitation of God's Names.

It is hard to find in the Qur'an, the Sunna, and the books of the early righteous scholars anything more strongly recommended than the recitation of God's Names. From daily prayers to holy struggle in His way, it is like the soul or blood of all worship. The profundity of recitation is proportional to the depth of feeling for God. Sufis call this "peace of heart" or" witnessing."

Some mention God Almighty and reach Him in their hearts via a mysterious way; others know Him through their consciences and feel His constant company by means of the point of

---

[141] Muslim, "Iman," 234.

reliance upon Him and seek His help in their inner worlds. Since they remember Him uninterruptedly, always mentioning Him with their heart and conscience, always feeling Him in their being, and living fully aware of His constant Presence, they regard mentioning Him verbally as being a sign of heedlessness and ignorance of Him. One who has reached this degree of *dhikr* says: *God knows that I do not remember Him to mention Him just now. How should I remember and mention Him now, given that I have never forgotten Him?*

Ihsan (Perfect Goodness)

Ihsan has two literal meanings, doing something well and perfectly and doing someone a favor; it is sometimes used in the Qur'an and the Sunna with either meaning. At other times, as pointed out in the reflections on *Heart - 2* while describing Prophet Joseph's consciousness of *ihsan*, it is used to encompass both meanings.

According to truth-seeking scholars, perfect goodness is an action of the heart that involves thinking according to the standards of truth; forming the intention to do good, useful things and then doing them; then performing acts of worship in the consciousness that God sees them. To attain perfect goodness, an initiate must establish his or her thoughts, feelings, and concepts on a firm belief, and then deepen that belief by practicing the essentials of Islam and training his or her heart to receive Divine gifts and be illuminated by the light of His manifestations. Only one who has attained such a degree of perfect goodness can really do good to others just for the sake of God, without expecting anything in return.

According to a Prophetic saying, *perfect goodness is that you worship God as if you were seeing Him; for even if you do not see Him, He certainly sees you.*[142] The most comprehensive and precise meaning of perfect goodness is that there is no fault in an initiate's action, and that he or she is always conscious that God is always watching. An initiate must concentrate on his or her actions with all of his or her will, feelings, awareness, and outer and inner senses. An initiate who is aware of God's supervision to this degree, and who therefore strives to act in the

---

[142] Al-Bukhari, "Iman," 37; Muslim, "Iman," 7; Abu Dawud, *Sunan*, 16.

best way possible, cannot help but do good to others. Doing good to others then becomes an essential attribute of his or her nature, and radiates as light radiates from the Sun.

Ihsan, in the sense of doing good to others, is summed up in the Prophet's principle of desiring for one's fellow Muslim whatever one desires for oneself.[143] Its universal dimension is defined in the Prophetic Tradition:

> Surely, God has decreed that you excel in whatever you do. When you punish someone by killing, do it kindly; when you slaughter an animal, slaughter it kindly. Let him who will slaughter it sharpen his knife and avoid giving the animal much pain.[144]

Consciousness of goodness is like a mysterious key that opens the door of a virtuous circle. An initiate who opens that door and steps into that illuminated corridor enters the "spiral" of a mysterious ascension, as if stepping onto an escalator. In addition to being endowed with this virtue, the correct use of one's free will to do good and refrain from evil will result in an advance of two steps for each step taken: *Is the reward of goodness anything but goodness?* (55:60). As we read in Tabari:

> Once God's Messenger, upon him be peace and blessings, he who was truthful and confirmed, asked his Companions about the verse: *Do you know what Your Lord means by this verse?* The Companions answered: *God and His Messenger know better.* He explained: *The reward of the one upon whom I conferred belief in Divine Unity and goodness is nothing but Paradise.*[145]

When the consciousness of goodness invades one's heart like clouds of rain, Divine favors begin to pour down. The possessor of such a heart, addressed by the verse: *For those who do good is the greatest good, and even more* (10:26), feels the profound pleasure of having been created as a human being.

---

[143] Al-Bukhari, "Iman," 7; Muslim, "Iman," 71.

[144] Muslim, "Sayd," 57; Al-Tirmidhi, "Diyat," 14.

[145] See the interpretation of *Surat al-Rahman* in Abu Ja'far Muhammad ibn Jarir al-Tabari, *Jami' al-Bayan fi Tafsir al-Qur'an,* 30 vols. (Beirut: Dar al-Ma'rifa, n.d.).

In addition to the blessings of Divine grace in return for good actions, Divine gifts issue from God's Graciousness and Kindness in return for a heart's sincere intention. We are unable to conceive of or describe such gifts.

A sound heart leads one straight to God without any deviation, and goodness is the heart's greatest and most rewarding action. Goodness is the safest way to ascend the slopes of sincerity, the most secure means to reach the peaks of being approved by God, and the consciousness of self-possession before the Eternal Witness. Of the many people equipped with belief, as well as deep fear and reverence for Him, who have taken the wings of good action and set out toward Him, only a few succeed in reaching the peak. May those who have not yet reached it try their utmost to do so. Those who have reached the peak feel deeply the ugliness of whatever God dislikes and are immune to it, while they are ready to do whatever He likes and to adopt such as their second nature.

Basira and *Firasa* (Insight and Discernment)

Literally meaning perception, intelligence, discretion, evidence, and witness, insight (*basira*) is defined as having an eye of the heart open, deep perception, an ability to see consequences at the beginning of an act, or foresight. Insight acquires a different, deeper dimension among Sufis. It is considered the sole source of spiritual knowledge obtained through reflective thought and inspiration, the first degree in the spirit's perception of the reality of things; and a power of conscience that discerns and establishes values originating in the spirit, whereas reason becomes entangled in colors, forms, and qualities. It is also a power of perception so sharpened by the light of nearness to the Divine Being that, when other powers of perception become exhausted by the imagination, it acquires great familiarity with mysteries lying behind things and, without any guide or evidence, reaches the Truth of the Truths, where reason is bewildered.

Seeing is one of the luminous Attributes of God Almighty, and one's insight, as declared in: *We have shared among them* (43:32), is proportionate to one's ability to receive the manifestations of this Attribute. The greatest portion belongs to the one who, having benefited from that Divine Source to the fullest, poured his inspirations into the hearts of his followers, namely Prophet Muhammad, upon him be peace and blessings. He is the most polished mirror of the manifestations of the Truth, and is unequaled in receiving them. The Divine declaration: *Say: This is my path. I call to God on clear evidence and by insight, I and whoever follows me* (12:108) points to the greatness of the share of that Divine gift belonging to the prince of the Prophets and his followers.

This matchless perceptiveness allowed that holy traveler on

the path of Ascension to reach in one breath the realms beyond corporeal existence, which those devoid of even the least perception regard as dark or unknown or the existence of which they categorically deny. He studied those realms like a book, and traveled on the "slopes" of the Unseen where the archetypal tablets are exhibited and the melodies of the pens of Destiny, which make one's heart jump, thrilled him. He visited Paradise accompanied by heavenly servants, and received a Divine welcome at a distance of no more than the distance between *the two bows' length, or even nearer* (53:9), at a point where space and location are undefined or undifferentiated.

The pleasure of observance given by insight sometimes acquires a new, deeper dimension when the believer begins to discern and discover the spiritual dimension and meanings of objects and events. His or her spirit experiences other dimensions in this three-dimensional realm, and his or her conscience becomes the eye of existence with which it sees, as well as its pulse and intellect.

In addition to perception and understanding, discernment (*firasa*) denotes the deepening of insight when perception becomes a source of certain knowledge. Those who discern the manifestations of the light of God, the Truth, possess such a radiance that they see everything, every issue, in its full clarity. They are never confused, even when encountering the most intricate elements, elements that are extremely similar, and do not become lost in particularities. Simultaneously seeing the sugar contained within the sugarcane and the hydrogen and oxygen contained within the water molecule, they refrain from all deviations (e.g., pantheism and monism) and recognize the Creator as He is, and the created as it is.

From the face of each individual believer to the face of the universe, every point, word, and line in existence is a meaningful sentence, even a book for those to whom the verse: *Surely in this are signs for those having insight and discernment* (15:75) refers. Those who can look at existence from the point stated in the Prophetic Tradition of: *Fear the discernment of a believer, for he*

sees with the light of God,[146] make contact with reality, become
familiar with the invisible side of existence, and shed light on
events, revealing the true face of everything. While others spend
their lives in "black holes," these people are enraptured with
increasing pleasures on Paradise-like "slopes."

For one endowed with such discernment, existence is a book
of countless pages, with each animate or inanimate part of
creation being a word shining with thousands of meanings, and
the face of existence and that of each person expressing many
hidden realities. Those of true spirituality see such things in the
"verses" of that book and in the luminous "phrases" of those
verses, and receive from them messages that even the greatest
minds among the non-believers are unable to discern. The
unimaginable surprises awaiting believers in the other world are
according to the rank of each, and are revealed to them along
with all the spiritual pleasure that they give.

---

[146] Al-Tirmidhi, "Tafsir al-Qur'an," 6.

Sakina and *Itmi'nan* (Serenity and Peacefulness)

Literally meaning calmness, silence, steadiness, solemnity, familiarity, the subsidence of the waves and tranquillity, *sakina* (serenity) is the opposite of flightiness, restlessness, wavering or indecision. In the language of Sufism, serenity means that a heart gradually comes to rest as a result of experiencing gifts from the Unseen. Such a restful heart always expects breezes to come from the realms beyond, and thus travels around in a state of *itmi'nan* (peacefulness), always careful and self-possessed. This rank is the lowest step of the rank of certainty that comes from direct observance. The resulting confusion over gifts coming through knowledge with gifts "obtained" through insight clouds the horizon when observing secret truths, giving rise to incorrect conclusions about the reality of things.

Serenity sometimes comes in the form of perceptible or imperceptible signs; at other times it appears so clearly that even ordinary people can identify it. Sometimes serenity and its signs resemble a spiritual breath or a Divine breeze that can be perceived only with great care; at other times, they come miraculously and so clearly that anyone can see them, as in the case of the Children of Israel during the time of Prophet Moses, and remain for some time among those deserving to be rewarded or equipped with them. One example is the substance that resembled vapor or mist surrounding Usayd ibn Khudayr while he was reading the Qur'an.[147] Such events are considered manifestations sent to strengthen the believers' willpower, to affirm their belief and hearten them.

---

[147] Usayd bin Khudayr felt surrounded by a vapor-like mass while reading the Qur'an and felt greatly exhilarated.

In either case, serenity is a Divine confirmation for those believers aware of their helplessness and destitution before God, a means of thankfulness and enthusiasm, as stated in: *He it is Who sent down serenity into the hearts of the believers so that they may have more faith added to their faith* (48:4). A believer gifted with serenity is not shaken by worldly fear, grief, or anxiety, and finds peace, integrity, harmony between his or her inner world and the outer world. Such a person is dignified, balanced, confident, assured and solemn, and self-possessed and careful in his or her relations with God Almighty. Egoism, vanity, and pride are abandoned; every spiritual gift received is attributed to God; humility and self-discipline are exhibited while thanking Him; and all dissatisfaction and uneasiness is ascribed to personal weakness and examined in the light of self-criticism.

As for peacefulness, it is defined as full satisfaction and the state of being at complete rest without any serious lapse. It is a spiritual state beyond serenity. If serenity is the beginning of being freed from theoretical knowledge and awakened to the truth, peacefulness is the final point or station.

The ranks or stations of *radiya* (being pleased with God in resignation) and *mardiya* (being approved by God) are two dimensions of peacefulness belonging to good and virtuous believers and are the depths of resignation. The ranks of *mulhama* (being inspired by God) and *zakiya* (being purified by God) are two other difficult-to-perceive degrees of peacefulness relating to those brought near to God. The gifts coming through them are pure and abundant.

Some thoughts and inclinations displeasing to God may appear in serene souls, while only perfect calmness is found in those that are peaceful and at rest. Peaceful hearts always seek God's pleasure or approval, and the "compass needle" of their conscience never swerves. Peacefulness is such an elevated rank of certainty that a soul traveling through it sees in every station the truth of: *I wish to set my heart at rest* (2:260) and is rewarded with gifts. Wherever the believer is, the breeze of: *No fear shall come upon them, neither shall they grieve* (2:62) is felt; the good tidings of: *Fear not, nor grieve, but rejoice in the good news of Paradise that has been promised to you* (41:30) is heard; the sweet, life-giving water of: *Beware, in the remembrance of God do hearts find peace and tranquility* (13:28) is tasted; and corporeality is defeated.

Peacefulness is realized when believers transcend material causes and means. Reason's transnatural journey ends at this point, and spirits are freed from worldly anxieties. Here, feelings find whatever they seek and become as deep, wide, and peaceful as a calm ocean. Those who have acquired this rank find the greatest peace only in feeling the company of God. They become aware of Divine Beauty and Grace in their hearts, feel attracted toward Him in order to meet with Him, are conscious that existence subsists by God's existence, and that the power of speech exists only because He has Speech. Through this opened window they acquire, despite their finitude, the power to see and hear in an extremely broad capacity. In the whirl of the most complicated events, where everyone else is bewildered and falters, such people travel in safety and escape the whirl.

In addition to being freed from worldly anxieties, a believer whose heart is at rest or peace welcomes with a smile both death and the obstacles following death, and hears the Divine compliments and congratulations: *Return to your Lord, pleased and well-pleasing. Enter among My servants, and enter My Garden* (89:29-30).

Death is seen as the most agreeable and desired result of life. When his or her life has ended in death, he or she hears, as was heard from the grave of Ibn 'Abbas, in every station passed through after death, the same Divine congratulations or Decree: *Return to your Lord, pleased and well-pleasing. Enter among My servants, and enter My Garden.*

Such people spend their lives in the grave on the "shores" of Paradise, experience the Great Gathering in wonder and admiration, the Supreme Weighing of Men's Deeds in awe and amazement, pass over the Bridge, only because they have to pass over it, and finally reach Paradise—the last, eternal abode of those whose hearts are at rest or have found peace and tranquillity. For such a person, the world is an 'Arafat[148] prepared on the way leading to the eternal forgiveness of the believers. The worldly life is the eve of the festival, and the other life is the festival day.

---

[148] The hill where Muslim pilgrims stay for some time on the eve of the Religious Festival of Sacrifice.

Qurb and *Bu'd* (Nearness and Remoteness)

Nearness (*qurb*) means that one transcends corporeality in order to acquire perfect spirituality and proximity to God. Some interpret this as God's proximity to His servants; however, this is not accurate. God is near to His servants, but not in terms of quantity or quality. Nearness in Sufi usage pertains to and is acquired by mortal beings, beings that are created in any phase or part of time, and undergoing different stages of existence. God's nearness to His creatures or bringing them near to Him is eloquently summed up in: *He is with you wherever you may be* (57:4). Such nearness is not the particular nearness acquired by belief and good deeds; it is God's being near to His servants, nearer to them than their own selves, including every created thing or being—living or non-living, believer or unbeliever, good or evil.

While general nearness, meaning God's nearness to the creation, encompasses everything and every person, particular nearness depends on belief and can be acquired by doing whatever God has decreed as good and right. This nearness to the Almighty is possessed by those who have discovered the way of nearness and, having entered the corridor leading to eternity, reach every morning and evening with a new, deep dimension of belief. Such people are included in the meaning of: *God is with those who keep from evil in reverence for God, and are doers of good* (16:128). Those who have obtained this rank recite: *Surely my Lord accompanies me and will guide me* (26:62) while inhaling, and: *Surely God is with us* (9:40) while exhaling.

In particular, nearness, consciousness of belief and perfect goodness have the same worth and significance as light does to seeing and soul does to body. Performing obligatory and supererogatory religious duties with this consciousness are like wings of light that carry one toward the "skies" of infinitude. The safest, most acceptable, and direct way of nearness to God is performing obligatory religious duties; however, performing supererogatory religious duties, which have no limit and show loyalty and devotion to God, results in true nearness and the rank of being loved by God Almighty.

A traveler to God enters new corridors leading to eternity on the wings of supererogatory duties, and feels rewarded with new Divine gifts, which engender an even greater desire to perform obligatory and supererogatory duties. One awakened to this truth feels in his or her conscience the love of God in direct proportion to his or her love of God. As stated in a *hadith qudsi* [149] :

> My servant cannot get near to Me through anything more lovable to Me than doing the obligatory religious duties. However, by doing supererogatory duties he gets nearer to Me, and when he becomes near to Me, I shall be his eyes to see with, his ears to hear with, his hands to grasp with, and his legs to walk on.

In short, such a believer is directed to act by the Divine Will.

Nearness acquired through performing obligatory duties is another title of the rank of one's being loved by God and included among the ones loved by God. As for nearness acquired through performing supererogatory duties, this is the rank of all one's acts being ascribed to God. It is a particular Divine bestowal and honor, as pronounced in: *You (Believers) slew them not, but God slew them. And you (Muhammad) did not throw when you threw, but God threw* (8:17).

Nearness, a particular gift of God, cannot be credited to one's actions without considering its Divine origin. Nearness to Him originates in His Greatness and Mercy, and remoteness from Him is one of the weaknesses and "abysses" of our character or nature. The writer of *Gülistan* (The Rose Garden) aptly expresses the origin of nearness and remoteness:

---

[149] A Prophetic Tradition whose meaning belongs directly to God and the wording to the Prophet.

The Friend is nearer to me than myself;
How strange it is that I am remote from Him.
What can I say and what can I do, that
While He is with me, I am distant from Him.

Remoteness means being distant from God and perishing. According to Sufis, the first indication of remoteness is the cessation of Divine gifts, and the final indication is that if a particular Divine help does not come, the person seeking it is completely lost and perishes. Just as degrees of nearness are based on whether one is an ordinary believer, a saint, a good and righteous person, or one brought near to God, remoteness also has its degrees in a line descending to Satan, who occupies the lowest point.

Nearness to God is a Divine favor, and remoteness from him is a deprivation. However, one cannot always feel his or her personal nearness to or remoteness from Him. The greatest favor of God is that He does not allow one to feel His (special) favor (e.g., being a saint or near to Him), lest the believer thus honored should feel pride and lose such favor. As a result, those nearest to God are usually unaware of their nearness. However, one's unawareness of his or her personal remoteness from God is a Divine reprisal. There are still others who, intoxicated with the love of God and making no distinction between nearness and remoteness, neither show desire for nearness nor worry over remoteness. The following couplet expresses the thoughts of such intoxicated souls:

Jami, worry yourself about neither nearness nor remoteness;
There is neither nearness nor remoteness, nor union nor parting.

It is an acknowledged fact that remoteness denotes horror and deprivation. However, some shiver due to the winds of awe blowing from nearness and feel themselves caught in the clutches of Divine wrath and destruction. The saying, *Nearness to the King is a burning fire* may express this mood. Nevertheless, if nearness may be likened to the slopes of Paradise that open to breezes of Divine familiarity and friendship, remoteness should be regarded as the abyss of deprivation and loss.

Ma'rifa (Spiritual Knowledge of God)

Ma'rifa literally denotes skill or talent, a special ability that belongs to certain people, and knowing by certain means. According to travelers on the path of God, it is the station where knowing is united with the one who knows, where knowing becomes second nature, and where each state reveals what or who is known. Some have defined ma'rifa as the appearance and development of the knowledge of God in one's conscience, or knowing God by one's conscience. In other words, one has attained self-realization and has realized his or her humanity with all of its intrinsic values and dimensions. This may be what is meant by: *The one who knows himself knows his Lord.*[150]

The first rank of ma'rifa is discerning the manifestations of the Divine Names surrounding us, and traveling in the amazing climate of the Attributes behind the door of mystery, half-opened by these manifestations. During this journey, lights flow continuously from the traveler's eyes and ears to his or her tongue, and one's heart begins to direct those acts that serve as a tongue confirming and proclaiming the Truth. This tongue becomes, so to speak, a diskette of "good words," and various lights from the light-giving truth of: *Unto Him good words ascend, and the righteous deed causes them to rise* (35:10) begin to be reflected on the screen of his or her conscience.

One who has acquired such ma'rifa is immune to all evil and is enveloped by breezes blowing from the realms beyond. Corridors of light are opened from his or her spirit toward the One known by the heart; Ibrahim Haqqi of Erzurum allegorically stated : *God said: I can be contained by neither the heavens nor*

---

[150] Al-'Ajluni, *Kashf al-Khafa'*, 2:262.

Earth. He is known by the heart as if a hidden treasure in the heart. The traveler is so enraptured with observing such scenes that he or she does not think of returning to a normal life.

A traveler who is completely closed to all else save God, who has resisted all corporeal desires and impulses in order to be carried by the tides of peace, has reached the stage of *ma'rifa*. One who travels around this point is called a traveler to *ma'rifa*; one who has reached it is called an *'arif* (a Gnostic, or one who has spiritual knowledge of God).

The differences found in commentaries on *ma'rifa* are based on the temperaments and schools of thought or levels of the Gnostics. Some have sought *ma'rifa* in the Gnostics themselves, and have seen the feeling of awe observed in them as the manifestation of *ma'rifa*. Others have seen it as connected with serenity, and judge the former's depth according to the latter's profundity; they have seen it as the heart's complete closure to everything but God; or they have understood it as the heart's wonder and admiration amidst the tides of Divine manifestations. Such hearts always beat with wonder and amazement, for the eyes of their owners open and close with amazement, and their tongues pronounce with wonder and admiration: *I acknowledge that I am unable to praise You as You praise Yourself.*[151]

With the spirit always flying upward toward eternity, and the heart enraptured with the pleasure of finding peace or being at rest, but always self-possessed and cautious, a life lived in *ma'rifa* is as calm and peaceful as that lived in the gardens of Paradise. Side-by-side with the angels, those who have acquired *ma'rifa* are included in the meaning of: *They do not disobey God in whatever He commands them, and carry out what they are commanded* (66:6). With feelings that are like buds waiting for daylight to blossom, such souls open fully with *ma'rifa* in "daylight" and experience the pleasure of intimacy with Him at every moment with a new dimension of *ma'rifa*. So long as they

---

[151] Muslim, "Salat," 222; Abu Dawud, "Salat," 148.

keep their eyes fixed on the door of the Truth, they are intoxicated by meeting with Him several times a day or even every
hour, and are enraptured with a new manifestation at every
moment.

While those supposing themselves to be scholars continue to
"crawl," and philosophers continue to philosophize and struggle
to build on the information they have, an *'arif* (one who has
attained knowledge of God) always tastes peace and talks about
peace in an effusion of "light." Even when others quake with
fear and awe of the Almighty, an *'arif* feels infinite pleasure and,
while his or her eyes weep, his or her heart smiles.

There are differences of manners and tendencies among *'arifs*
based on temperaments and schools of spiritual training. While
some are deep and silent, like whirlpools, and thus hard to identify
because of their simple, quiet appearance, others "gurgle" like
waterfalls. Some always weep for fear of committing sins and
their inability to do a single good thing, and never tire of praising
their Lord; others continuously travel in awe, modesty, and
familiarity and never think of leaving this "ocean". Still others are
like the earth which everybody else "treads", as no one shows
them respect or thinks that they are *'arifs*; or they are like clouds
sending "water" to everyone under them, or like breezes, for they
touch our feelings and blow us good and favor.

An *'arif* can be recognized in several ways: such a person
expects favor from and becomes intimate only with the Known
One; he or she lifts his or her eyelids and opens the doors of his
or her heart only to Him; he or she turns only to Him in love;
and experiences the greatest suffering when anyone other than
Him is desired. One who has not acquired true knowledge of
God Almighty cannot distinguish between the Beloved and
others, and one who is not intimate with the Beloved cannot
know separation's torment and pain.

Mahabba (Love)

Mahabba means fondness, tender and kind feelings, preference, and love. Love that affects and invades one's feelings is called passion; love that is so deep and irresistible that it burns for union[152] is called fervor and enthusiasm. Sufis have defined love as the relation of the heart with the Truly Beloved One, the irresistible desire felt for Him, the struggle to comply with His desires or commandments in all acts and thoughts, and the state of being enraptured and intoxicated without "sobriety" until the time of union or re-union. These definitions can be summed up as "standing" in the Presence of God, as being freed from all transient relationships and worries.

True love means that a lover is set wholly on the Beloved, is always and inwardly with Him, and never has any other desire or wish. The heart of a person who has such a degree of love always beats with a new contemplation for the Beloved at every moment. His or her imagination always travels in His mysterious climate, his or her feelings receive new messages from Him at every moment, his or her will takes wings with these messages, and he or she passionately desires to meet Him.

---

[152] "Union," in Sufi terminology, should not be confused with communion with or participation in the Divine Being, as in some philosophies or mistaken Gnostic traditions. The fundamental relation between God and humanity, regardless of whether that person is the greatest of humanity, namely, Prophet Muhammad, upon him be peace and blessings, is the relation of the Creator to the created. In the Sufi context, union means coming together again after parting. The world is the realm of separation for humanity, and all men and women burn inwardly with the desire to return to their true home. This return will be realized when the person dies, for that is the beginning of his or her passage into the other world. Although a Sufi finds God in his or her heart while in this world, true re-union will only take place in the Hereafter in Paradise.

While a lover who transcends his or her self with the wings of love and reaches the Lord at the points of passion and enthusiasm, and carries out his or her responsibilities toward the King of his or her heart in such a condition, the heart of that lover is set on His vision. Such a believer's nature is "burned" with the light of Divine Grandeur, and lost in wonder and amazement. With the cup of love on one's lips, while the veils of the Unseen are lifted one after the other, he or she becomes intoxicated with studying the meanings that come in rays from behind those veils, and is enraptured with the pleasure of watching the scenes behind them. One's walking and stopping occur at the command of God, speech is no more than the inspiration that comes from Him, and silence, when observed, is done in His name. At various times, he or she journeys toward Him in "His company," or is occupied with communicating His message to others.

Some have defined love, in the context of God's love of His distinguished servants, as doing good, and as obedience, devotion, and unconditional submission in the context of a servant's love of God. The following couplets of the female Sufi saint Rabi'a al-'Adawiya are significant in expressing this meaning:

> You talk about loving God while you disobey Him;
> I swear by my life that this is something very strange.
> If you were truthful in your love, you would obey Him,
> For a lover obeys whom he loves.

Love is based on two important pillars: that which is manifested by the lover's acts (a lover tries to comply with the Beloved's desires), and the lover's inner world (a lover should inwardly be closed to anything not related to Him). Real men and women of God mean this when they talk about love. According to them, emotional concern with or love of any kind of pleasure, including spiritual, cannot be called "love" in its true sense. It can only be figurative love.

Every lover cannot feel the same degree of love for the Beloved, for love varies according to the lover's spiritual and emotional depth, the degree of consciousness of and care in obedience to the Beloved. For example, the love felt by those beginning the way is not established and constant. They dream of acquiring the rank of perfect goodness and, at times, receive signs of the Knowledge of God, thrill at the twinkle of the "light" appearing on their horizon, and vaguely feel amazement and wonder.

On the other hand, those who have made great progress fly in the heaven of love toward the highest point. They live in the bright climate of the Qur'an as embodiments and examples of the good morals of Prophet Muhammad, upon him be peace and blessings. While trying to represent his good morals, they expect no material or spiritual reward and demand no pleasure. Even at the summit of this holy representation, like fruit-bearing trees whose branches bend with the weight of their fruit, they lower their wings of humility and always mention the Beloved. If they are shaken with a fault or error, they severely criticize and fight with themselves.

And finally, those most advanced in the love of God are like rain clouds in the "heaven" of Islam. They feel all existence with Him, live with Him, and see and breathe with Him. In a never-ending cycle, they are filled with pangs of separation (from Him) and a desire to meet Him; when relieved or emptied, they mount on a beam of light and descend to Earth to embrace the whole of existence.

One who turns to Him with heartfelt desire and sincere enthusiasm, regardless of the degree of love, receives a reward according to the depth of feeling and concern for Him. The first group of people mentioned above receive special favor and mercy. The second group of people reach the horizon of perceiving the Attributes of Grace and Majesty, and are freed from defects of character. Those of the third group are illumined by the light of His Being, awakened to the reality of things, and are in touch with the dimension of existence behind veils. That is, the Almighty manifests the light of His Grandeur to burn up the corporeal attributes of those whom He loves and elevates them to the realm of Divine Attributes, such as the All-Seeing and All-Hearing. He awakens them fully to the fact that they are poor and helpless before Him, and fills their hearts with the light of His existence.

One whose love has reached this degree, and who is rewarded with so much Divine favor, attains an eternal life beyond existence or non-existence. Like a bar of iron put into fire and thus appearing as a bar of fire, such a lover may be unable to distinguish the Divine Being and His manifestations, and therefore expresses feelings and experiences in terms associated with such false beliefs as incarnation and union (with God). In such circumstances, one must consider the Sunna's established criteria.

The expressions uttered by profoundly spiritual individuals lost in and intoxicated with love of God cannot be used as the criteria by which to judge them. Otherwise, we may feel enmity toward such friends of God, who are favored with His continuous company according to the Prophetic Tradition: *A man is with him whom he loves*,[153] and, as declared in the *hadith qudsi*: *Whoever becomes an enemy of My friends has waged war on Me.*[154]

---

[153] Al-Tirmidhi, "Zuhd," 50.
[154] Al-Bukhari, "Riqaq," 38.

'Ashq (Passion or Intense, Ecstatic Love)

'Ashq means intense love of and fondness for perfection, beauty, or physical charm. Sufis usually call this sort of love, for example, love for the opposite sex, figurative or metaphorical love. Real love, the love of the Eternal Monarch, is felt for His Grace and Beauty manifested within His Majesty, and for His Majesty manifested within His Grace and Beauty. The real, intense love felt for God is a wing of light granted to us by Him so that people can use it to reach Him. Feeling such love can also be viewed as the spirit being like a moth drawn toward the Light, the essence of existence. This intense love is the most basic and mysterious cause of the universe's creation. God has created the universe in order to be known and loved, and so that those souls awakened to truth will feel and manifest a deep interest in His Essence, the Attributes, and Names.

'Ashq, which the spirit feels without the intervention of free will, cannot be controlled by the person so affected, for its real source is God, Who loves Himself in a way special to His Sacred Essence and is essentially independent of the created. In addition, it is essentially different from the love felt by the created for the created or the Creator. This sacred, essential love of God for Himself, including His Attributes and Names, is the reason why He created the universe and why He caused humanity to appear in the world. It is also this love that manifests itself in human beings as love for God, as the most essential center of humanity's relationship with God.

'Ashq is the final step leading to God, and a lover who has reached it almost has no further steps to take. God manifested Himself first as this sacred, essential love required by His being God. I particularly avoid attributing to Him 'ashq (passion or esctatic love) in the absolute sense of the word, and prefer using the word *mahabba* (love).

Some tend to call this Divine Love Knowledge, as Knowledge is the first manifestation of the Absolute Divine Being, Who is infinitely exalted above having any equals or likes. Every manifestation of the Divine Being is a condescension. This first condescension is called "Knowledge," as it is God's manifestation of His Knowledge. It is also called "the Sacred Love" in the sense that God loves to observe and to be "observed;" or "the Tablet" as it comprehends or contains all of existence; or "the Pen," as it handles all things in existence in all their details. *Jabarut* (the highest, immaterial empyrean) and the Truth of Ahmad (the Prophet's Name mentioned in the original copy of the Gospels and in the heavens) are other titles of this condescension, or the first manifestation of the Divine Being.

Sacred Love is a mystery peculiar to the Divine Essence. Other Attributes of His are appended to or dependent on this love. It is for this reason that those who fly with the wings of *'ashq* directly reach the Divine Essence and attain amazement, whereas others have to pass through the intermediate realms of the worlds of things and Names.

* * *

The ways leading to God are almost beyond number. Sufism, the science of truth, contains the food, light, and other necessities travelers need for the journey, and the (spiritual) orders (*tariqas*) are the ports from which they set out, or the schools in which the principles of the journey are taught.

The ways to the Truth can be divided into two main groups. The first is the way in which the wayfarer is offered or taught such principles as eating less, drinking less, sleeping less, increasing contemplation, and refraining from unnecessary social intercourse. Almost all Sufi orders are based on these practices. The main invocations recited by followers of this way are the Seven Names: There is no god but God, God, He, the Truth, the All-Living, the Self-Subsistent, the All-Overwhelming. By reciting these Names, one seeks to pass through the seven steps of the human self or soul: the Evil-Commanding, the Self-Condemning, the Inspired, the Serene and Peaceful or the Soul at Rest, the Content (with however God treats it), the (Soul) Pleasing (to God), and the Purified or Innocent Self or Soul. To these seven Names, some add such Names of Majesty as the All-Powerful, the All-Strong, the All-Compelling, the Master, and the All-Loving; others add such Names of Grace as the Unique, the One, the Peerlessly All-Single, and the Eternally Besought-of-All.

The second way is based on strict adherence to the Qur'an and the Sunna, and the encouragement of certain recitations. Those who follow this way strive to comply with the Sunna in whatever they do. Rather than reciting certain Names, they follow the methods used by God's Messenger to worship, invoke, and pray, reflect on His acts and creatures, and mention Him with all of His Names. Joining these activities with a meticulous following of the commandments of Shari'a, they are firmly attached to their guides or teachers and abandon themselves to the tides of *'ashq* and spiritual attraction toward God.

Once they have attained *'ashq* and attraction, existence with its outer dimension vanishes from their sight. They are annihilated with respect to the carnal aspect of their existence and begin to feel and observe the absolute Divine Unity. At this point, they immediately come to their senses without becoming confused or going to extremes in the relationship between the Creator and the created. In such a manner do they complete their journey.

The basic principles of this second way are regular worship, love, spiritual attraction toward God, regular recitation, and the companionship of one's guide or teacher. In this context recitation, in addition to mentioning God with all of His Names, involves study or attending classes in whatever leads one to God. This is what the Prophet, upon him be peace and blessings, meant when he described those with whom God is pleased: *They study together*.

At times, a lover finds himself or herself in the stream of joyful zeal and yearning, which can be regarded as another dimension of *'ashq*.

Shawq and *Ishtiyaq* (Joyful Zeal and Yearning)

Literally meaning strong desire, excessive yearning, joy issuing from knowing, delight, and longing, *shawq* (joyful zeal) is used by Sufis to express the heart's overwhelming desire to meet with the Beloved, Who cannot be comprehended and "vanishes" after being "observed." Some have described this as joyful desire, excitement, and a lover's excessive heartfelt longing to see the Face of the Beloved. Others have regarded it as a fire that reduces to ashes all desires, wishes, yearnings, and inclinations other than those that strive to meet with the Beloved.

Joyful zeal originates in love. The remedy of a heart burning with such a longing to meet with the Beloved is meeting with Him, and *shawq* is the wing of light that carries the lover to this meeting. Zeal disappears when a lover finds the Beloved, while the yearning for Him (*ishtiyaq*) continues to increase. One who yearns for Him never stops yearning and, whenever favored with a special manifestation of His Essence, wishes for more. This is why the prince of the Prophets and the greatest of humanity, upon him be peace and blessings, who, equipped at each moment with a new radiance of knowledge, love of God, and spiritual delight, incessantly traveled between the summits of love, joyful zeal, and yearning, and used to pray: *O God! I ask You for zeal to observe Your perfectly beautiful Face and to meet with You.*[155]

Some interpreters of the Qur'an, when writing about: *Those who believe are firmer in love of God* (2:265) remark that joyful zeal is felt toward things that are partly perceivable and partly imperceivable, partly comprehensible and partly incomprehen-

---

[155] Nasa'i, "Sahw," 62; Ibn Hanbal, *Musnad*, 5:191.

sible. One feels no zeal toward that which he or she has never seen or heard of, or about which he or she knows nothing. Nor does he or she feel interest in that which he or she completely comprehends or perceives.

Zeal and yearning can be divided into two categories. The first is the yearning produced by separation from the Beloved after meeting with and gazing upon Him in the past eternity. The sighs uttered by the flute of Rumi, and the creaking, painful sounds heard by Yunus Emre from the revolving water-wheel express such a separation. These sighs will continue until the final union or meeting with Him.[156] The second category is when a lover sees the Beloved from behind a veil, and thus cannot completely comprehend Him. The believer feels His presence, but cannot see Him; he or she dips a finger into the honey of love but is not allowed to take a further step. Consumed with thirst, the believer cries: *I am being consumed with thirst! Give me some water!* but receives no answer.

The spirit of all men and women observed Him in an assembly of past eternity, where God asked them: *Am I not your Lord?* and they answered: *Yes, assuredly. We testify!* [157] After this

---

[156] Rumi says that notes of a flute are the groans of separation from the reed bed. For Yunus Emre, a Turkish folk poet of the thirteenth century, a revolving water-wheel's creaking sounds are groans of separation from the forest. Figuratively, both remind people of their separation from the Eternally Beloved One after their togetherness with Him in the "past eternity." This phrase has been coined to convey the meaning of the Arabic word '*azal*: the state of having no beginning).

The initial verses of al-Rumi's Mathnawi are:

> Hear from the flute, for it relates [what happened to it];
> It complains about separation.
> I seek a breast "cleft" because of separation
> So that I can unburden (to it) my zeal for re-union. (Trans.)

[157] This refers to the Qur'anic verse: *Remember when your Lord brought forth from the children of Adam, from their loins, their seed, and made them testify of themselves, (saying): "Am I not your Lord?" They said: "Yes, assuredly. We testify." That was lest you should say at the Day of Resurrection: "Of this we are unaware."* (7:172) (Trans.)

assembly, either because humanity's very humanness required it or because humanity had to be tested, to believe in Him without seeing Him, humanity was thrown into the pangs of temporary separation. This is why people always dream of Him in a conscious or unconscious longing for Him, and burn with a yearning to re-unite with Him. What is more significant than this is the yearning which the Most Sacred Being feels toward pure, innocent, and unadulterated souls, but only in a way that is appropriate for His essential independence of all being. This Divine eagerness may be the real source of the yearning that enters one's heart.

Zeal means turning to the Beloved with all inner and outer feelings, and locking out all appetites other than those one feels to meet with Him. In the context of yearning, it means one is overflowing with desires and wishes related to Him. Both zeal and yearning feed the spirit. Both are painful, but exhilarating, and distressing but promising.

No individual experiences more anguish, nor is none happier, than the one who burns with love and groans with zeal. Such people become so angelic when enraptured with the thought and hope of meeting with God that they would not agree to enter Paradise at that moment, even if allowed to do so. They burn inwardly with the pangs of separation to such a degree that even the waters of Paradise can not extinguish the fire in their hearts. Only meeting with the Friend can extinguish such a fire. Paradoxically, they never think of escaping that fire, for even if they were offered the sanctuary of the palaces of Paradise to prevent them from burning with the fire of zeal to meet with the Friend, such people would scream out like the inhabitants of Hell who seek to be rescued from Hellfire.

Worldly people cannot know what that zeal means or the state of those who possess it. People of zeal are amazed at worldly people, so engrossed in their worldly affairs and pleasures. Their amazement is quite natural, for God Almighty told Prophet David, upon him be peace:

O David! If those who love and show inclination to the world knew how much I care about them, want them to resist against sins, and how I expect to meet with human beings, they would be dying with the zeal to meet with Me.[158]

When the zeal to meet with God invades a lover's being, the result is an overflow of feelings of pain and delight and cries of:

> Zeal has bewildered me, zeal has burnt me.
> Zeal has intervened between sleep and my eyes.
> Zeal has invaded me, zeal has engrossed me.
> Zeal has overwhelmed me, zeal has stricken me with awe.

This degree of zeal sometimes incites the lover to stand up and dance or spin. The lover should be excused for such movements, as he or she cannot resist such a spiritual state:

> Say to him who wants to prevent a man of ecstasies from going into ecstasies:
> *You have not tasted the wine of love together with us, so leave us.*
> When souls overflow with the zeal to meet with the Beloved,
> Know, O you unaware of spirituality, that bodies begin to dance.
> O guide who incites lovers, stand up and move us
> With the name of the Beloved, and breathe life into us.

In our own day, some prefer to serve the Qur'an and faith by the way based on acknowledging one's poverty and impotence before God's Wealth and Power, and on thankfulness and zeal. In this context, zeal means constant hope and continuing to serve without becoming dispirited or losing one's energy. It also means seeking an aspect of Divine mercy even in the most distressing conditions, and then relying upon Him alone for His help and victory.

---

[158] Al-Qushayri, *Al-Risala*, 332.

Jadhb and *Injidhab* (Attraction and the Feeling of Being Attracted toward God)

In the language of Sufism, *jadhba* (attraction) means that a servant is attracted toward God by God Himself, purified thereby of human imperfection in spiritual elevation, and equipped with Divine Attributes or exalted morals as specified in the Qur'an. It also means feeling and observing clearly the manifestations of Divine Majesty and Unity. A purified soul capable of receiving such manifestations abandons itself to the tides originating from the realms beyond and, like a competent swimmer, swims in ecstasy, in deep submission to God and without fear and anxiety.

If attraction means that one is drawn by a sacred power linked with his or her essence toward the purpose of his or her creation and to the point indicated by his or her true, primordial nature, *injidhab* means the willing acceptance of this invitation to the spirit.[159]

Attraction is so great a Divine favor that it cannot be obtained through ordinary means or causes. It is God Himself Who grants to His pure-hearted servants both the attraction and the ability to receive it: *That is the grace of God: He bestows it on whom He wills* (57:21). This bestowal includes, in a single, passing moment, many portions of time filled with events, and it equips a single step toward Him with the potential to reach the gardens of Paradise, and a single glance with the capacity to turn

---

[159] According to Islam, every child is born sinless and with inborn capabilities, faculties, and nature to accept Islam and live according to it. This is called "primordial nature" (*fitra*). However, the adverse education he or she later receives, as well as the surrounding environment, greatly affect his or her choice.

a piece of coal into a diamond. Great distances that seem impossible to cover with one's own will and power are covered in a moment by God's attraction, and high summits are reached by His uplifting, as stated in: *A single instance of the All-Merciful's attraction equals to the nearness to God acquired through the good actions of both humanity and jinn.*[160]

Those whose spirits feel the mysteries of faith, who practice Islam and perfect goodness and devotion through God's attraction are called "those who follow the way of Uways,"[161] for they are taught directly by God or the Prophet. In other words, they do not need a teacher or guide except God and the Prophet. Since they feel continuously attracted toward God by God Himself, they live in incessant ecstasy and amazement at what they observe of the Divine truths and manifestations.

At times, there is a virtuous circle between attraction and regular worship and austerity. A traveler on the way to God is favored with attraction in proportion to the degree of his or her worship and austerity, and is devoted to worship and austerity to the extent of the attraction felt toward God. So long as such people act in accordance with the Shari'a, this virtuous circle continues. If they break away from the light of Muhammad, upon him be peace and blessings, displays of free and easy behavior in their relationship with God begin to appear, and religious obligations might begin to be neglected.

Attraction is, first of all, a capability and a Divine gift given in advance. Without this gift, a traveler on the way cannot feel attracted through austerity, worship, and self-purification; nor can he or she discern the waves of attraction and being attracted on the face of the universe produced by the light coming from the Divine Name the All-Loving. Such an undiscerning person has no knowledge of true spirituality:

---

[160] Al-'Ajluni, *Kashf al-Khafa'*, 1:332.

[161] Uways al-Qarani is regarded by some as the greatest Muslim saint of the first Islamic century.

> Why should my guide be concerned with me
> Unless I have the attraction of love?
> Why should he be concerned with me
> Unless I receive inspiration from God?

It sometimes happens that a believer attracted in this way is overwhelmed by the gifts coming from God, so that whatever is other than His manifestations disappears, and all cares with the world or the Hereafter are forgotten. In a mood expressed by the following couplet:

> I am, by nature, so attracted to the roaring rise of the sea
> That I feel as if engulfed in the bounteous gifts of God,

one's self and all other parts of creation are seen as being intoxicated with the attraction of the Holy, Attractive Being:

> Everything is intoxicated with the wine of love of God and the attraction of this love. Celestial objects and angels are intoxicated; the heavens and Earth are intoxicated; elements and plants are intoxicated; and animals, human beings, and all other beings (are intoxicated).[162]

There are two kinds of attraction. One is felt inwardly and is not manifested outwardly by its possessor. Such a person loves God, feels great contentment with and pleasure in fulfilling His commandments, and feels incessantly attracted to the source of a deeper delight. The second kind of attraction is that which is manifested. One who feels such attraction cannot help but manifest it as ecstasy. Feeling attracted by God with a continuously increasing force, he or she lives as an ecstatic, in excessive joy and with great happiness.

Those who are unaware of such degrees of spiritual elevation think such a person is crazy. The following couplet of 'Abd al-'Aziz Majdi Effendi expresses this degree of ecstasy quite meaningfully:

> There is a kind of madness called attraction, which is a true triumph.
> By means of it madness reaches mysteries lofty and great.

---

[162] Bediüzzaman Said Nursi, *The Words 2* (Izmir, Turkey: 1997), 346.

Attraction may look like madness in some respects; in reality, it is quite different. For example, an ecstatic who revolves in waves of attraction may lose some perception and show signs of madness by behaving in ways incompatible with sound reasoning and the Shari'a. In most cases, an ecstatic exceeds normal human standards in all senses or powers of perception to the extent that, in the light of Sunna, he or she travels in realms that cannot be reached by the reason, other intellectual faculties and senses of ordinary people. Therefore, those who see such a person think that he or she is crazy.

However, traveling (in spiritual realms) beyond the reach and power of normal standards of intellect or reason, by using that power and other senses along with the help of God, is completely different from the type of madness resulting from mental illness, which is characterized by less-than-normal standards of intellect or reason.

Dahsha and *Hayra*
(Utmost Astonishment and Amazement)

Every traveler journeying in the valleys of love and zeal some-times burns with the fire of love, and sometimes overflows with joy owing to the "wine of immortality" offered by the Beloved. While burning, the lover sighs: *O Cupbearer, I have burned away. Give me some water!* While looking attentively through the door of the Beloved left ajar, the lover entreats: *I have dipped my finger into the honey of love. Give me some water!*

Until the traveler is saved from worldly anxiety and consid-erations of distance or, in other words, until the traveler passes beyond the spheres of the manifestations of Names and Attri-butes and is honored with the manifestation of Divine Essence, he or she continues to travel between burning and entreating, and receiving his or her lot from *the pure drink the Lord offers* (76:21).

The lover pursues more and more knowledge of God, for every new Divine gift increases his or her desire. As this desire increases, new gifts pour into the lover's heart. He or she embroiders the acquired knowledge of God with the feelings and thoughts traveling between his or her heart and things. Like a honeybee collecting nectar from flowers and thus making flowers the source of honey, the lover collects the nectar of the knowledge of God from the manifestations of Divine Names and Attributes that open like flowers in the garden of the universe. He or she distills the collected nectar through the filter of his or her appreciative, grateful conscience, and feels as if his or her sight has reached the rays of the Attributes themselves. Then the dream of reaching the Divine Being is realized, and the lover is stricken with the utmost astonishment.

The writer of *Gülistan* (The Rose Garden) expresses the traveler's feelings of astonishment and amazement while burning and drinking:

At times You show Your Beautiful Face,
But It is veiled without being completely seen,
Thus You incite us to compete to be able to see You
And increase our fire.
When I see unveiled the Beloved
With Whom I have fallen in love,
Something occurs to me
And I am bewildered on my way.
The Beloved lights a fire in my breast
And then puts it out with a drizzle.
That is why you find me burnt away
And drowned in an ocean.

Bursawi presents travelers as incessantly intoxicated:

All saintly ones are intoxicated
with the pure water their Lord offers them (76:21);
Seven, five, and four are intoxicated
With His Beautiful Face.[163]

If the traveler has not prepared his or her heart according to the requirements of the spiritual journey and the commandments of the Shari'a (that is, if one does not think and reason in the light of the Prophethood while one's feelings fly in the boundless realm of the achieved spiritual state), he or she will inevitably fall, be confused and bewildered, and speak and act contrary to the spirit of the Shari'a.

Mulla Jami' expresses astonishment and amazement in his vivid language:

The women of Egypt were astounded and cut their hands when they saw the beauty of Joseph. O Master! If they had seen your beauty, they would have thrust the daggers in their hands into their breasts. Speaking of Joseph's beauty where Your beauty is mentioned, is no more than making up stories.

---

[163] Isma'il Haqqi Bursawi, *Tafsir Ruh al-Bayan*, 10 vols. (N.p.: Maktabat al-Islamiya, 1330 AH / 1911 CE), 10:276.

In other words, if transient, worldly beauty and perfection that only reflect the Infinitely Perfect and Beautiful One through many veils can seduce us, how great will be our inability to perceive the dazzling awe and amazement produced by beholding and gazing upon that Beauty.

Those who prefer to serve Islam and the Qur'an at this point in time should not aim at all the pleasures, whether bodily or spiritual. Rather, they should continue their service, assisted by God, in awe of and with amazement at the extent to which God comes to their aid and makes them successful. They should never conceive of anything other than serving Islam. This is a special gift of amazement to the army of light from God's special treasury of: *We make the distribution among them* (43:32).

Qabd and *Bast* (Contraction and Openness)

Qabd (contraction) and *bast* (openness), emotions felt by almost everyone during their lives, relate especially to those who live their lives consciously. Literally meaning being caught, being in straits or distressed and being grasped by the hand, Sufis use *qabd* to mean that the link between an individual and the source of his or her spiritual gifts and radiance has been severed for a certain period. This causes distress and makes one suffer from a spiritual obstruction and blockage. On the other hand, *bast* can be described as openness, expansion, development, relief, being freed from spiritual blockage, and developing inwardly or spiritually to the point that the seeker becomes a means of mercy and embraces all things or beings in existence.

Fear and hope or expectation are deliberate attitudes, and are a first station for a traveler on the way to God. Contraction and openness are mysterious "bargains" that have been made without the will or intention of the traveler. The first one blocks his or her way; the second one gives him or her wings to fly to the heights. If fear and hope represent anxiety about and the joy of expectations for the future, as well as liked and disliked things, contraction and openness can be regarded as the heart's contracting with gloom and depression and expanding with joy.

Contraction and openness have the same meaning for travelers on the slopes of knowledge of God as do fear and hope or expectation for the newly initiated. Both are in the hands of God, even if we cannot exclude from them part of one's free will: *God contracts and expands* (2:245). As the whole of existence is in His grasp and at His free disposal, it is He Who directs and disposes of all things, from the heavens to the human heart. The Prophetic saying: *The heart is between the two Fingers of the All-*

Merciful; He turns it from state to state and gives it whatever form He wishes reminds us of this fact.[164]

When God wills, He contracts a heart so tightly that only He can provide what will satisfy it. By contrast, He expands and exhilarates it to such an extent that it needs nothing. Contraction is caused by God's Majesty; openness is caused by His Grace. While the Grandeur and Magnificence relating to the manifestation by God of His Names on the whole of existence are displayed in the former, Mercy and Condescension are manifested in the latter. In the former, there is the frightening, awesome, and majestic nature of the Power that turns all existence from huge systems into particles, while in the latter there are affectionate breezes for those spirits trembling in awe at this infinitely vast, overwhelming Power, this overpowering Majesty.

Not everyone can feel such manifestations of Majesty and Grace at the same level, for the extent of contraction and openness is proportionate to one's emotional and spiritual capacity. What an ordinary person feels as distress and relief or rejoicing differs markedly from the spiritual joy and anxiety experienced by one awakened to the Divine truths, one who is ever-alert for what will come through the half-opened door from the realms beyond, and who is conscious of God's continuous and direct supervision.

Like every element of existence, contraction and openness are at the disposal of the Creator, Who alternates them continuously, like night and day. Even if this alternation appears to originate in the deeds performed in accordance with one's free will, the Divine Will extends or shortens the periods of contraction and openness, and causes one to be consumed with tension or to overflow with delight. Sometimes a lover experiences openness for a long time, feeling as if flying like a bird, without being touched by any form of contraction; other times, contraction is a constant companion that stays so long that the lover feels that he or she is going from one hardship to another (and greater) hardship.

---

[164] Ibn Hanbal, *Musnad*, 2:173; Al-Tabari, *Jami' al Bayan*, 3:126.

As neglecting the requirements of one's spiritual position bestowed by God causes contraction, sins usually come together with contraction. For this reason, a believer must always be alert against committing new sins and deviations while suffering contraction, must not be overpowered by heedlessness, and must strive for self-purification through sincere repentance and the performance of good deeds. Then, the believer must wait for what will come from the realms beyond.

While contraction is accompanied by fear, perplexity, and feelings of spiritual emptiness, openness manifests itself as joy, rapture, and feelings or utterances of pride. For this reason, openness may be risky for those spiritually less-developed people who have not yet attuned themselves to journeying in "celestial" realms.

Although there are risks associated with contraction, those associated with openness are greater and more numerous. One caught in contraction usually feels in his or her conscience an absolute need of the Almighty, and so turns to Him in sincere acknowledgment of this neediness with the words: *Hold me! Hold me, lest I should fall!* and, escaping the spiritual waste he or she feels, is favored with the Almighty's help and reaches those heights that are beyond reach during times of openness.

This is why some people are exposed to heedlessness and loss of spiritual energy during times of openness, and why contraction leads almost every believer to new levels of alertness. In addition, the contraction originating from our sins or neglect usually signals the beginning of a new wave of openness; similarly, an expansion that causes pride and loss of spiritual energy may give rise to a new contraction.

A true believer is one who can judge each state experienced or achieved as it really is, with all of its aspects, and make it fruitful. Contraction and openness are manifestations from Him for one who knows. He causes openness so that the servant will thank Him, and causes contraction so that the servant may become more alert.

Faqr and *Ghina* (Poverty and Richness)

For Sufis, poverty means that an initiate claims possession of nothing and is freed from all kinds of attachment toward worldly things, and that one feels total neediness and destitution before God in one's relationship with Him, which is based on servanthood and the fact that God is the Sole Object of Worship. It is not poverty as understood by ordinary people, nor does it mean begging from people, displaying one's privations.

The Sufi way of poverty involves severing relationships with all that is other than the Eternally Besought-of-All, and depending only on Him to meet one's needs. For this reason, the more detached one is from whatever is worldly and temporary and the more annihilated one is in depending on the Divine Attributes and Essence, the more one has attained poverty and can repeat the saying of the Prophet, upon him be peace and blessings: *Poverty is my pride.*[165]

As stated in a blessed saying, when poverty becomes a dimension of faith and submission, one no longer depends on the help, will, and power of that which is not God. Even if such a person has enough wealth to fill the whole world, as the world is subject to decay and exhaustion, one does not depend upon it, but rather turns to God with all of one's strength and feeling, conscious of his or her essential poverty and helplessness. How beautiful is the following couplet of Nabi, a seventeenth-century Ottoman poet:

> Do not despise poverty, O Nabi!
> Poverty is the mirror where the independence of others is reflected.

---

[165] Al-'Ajluni, *Kashf al-Khafa'*, 2:87.

Rumi made another fine observation about poverty:

> Poverty is the essence and all else is form;
> Poverty is a remedy and all else the disease.
> The whole world consists in vanity and conceit;
> But poverty is the real core and meaning of existence.

Even if a person cannot discern his or her essential weakness and poverty with the light of belief, it is a reality that he or she is weak, poor, and needy. God Almighty declares: *O mankind! You are poor in your relation with God, while God is He Who is the All-Wealthy and Worthy of Praise, Who returns abundantly whatever is done for Him* (35:15). As absolutely everybody needs His act of choice, will, and decree to come into existence, His Self-Subsistent and All-Subsisting Existence is also needed at every moment to survive.

An individual's poverty and neediness before the Almighty is not a means of humiliation; rather, one's increased awareness of one's poverty engenders higher degrees of dignity, for such awareness before the Absolutely Wealthy One is richness itself. The believer becomes aware of his or her non-dependence on others, and acquires the consciousness of independence to the extent that one feels in his or her conscience that God is the sole source of power and wealth. His help is sought, and it is therefore to Him that one turns. Even if such a person is materially poor, he or she feels no need for anything or anyone else.

The believer is convinced that whatever or whoever exists, including himself or herself, essentially belongs to the Almighty, for all elements of creation are only shadows of the shadow of His absolutely independent existence. This degree of conviction of God's Unity is called annihilation in God, two steps ahead of which is subsistence with God. Concerning this, Hayali says:

> Hayali, cover your naked body with the shawl of poverty;
> This is their pride, they know not of satin or silk.

Poverty is the goal of saints, the (natural) state of purified scholars, and the most manifest sign of love of God. The Almighty has placed poverty in the hearts of His friends so that those hearts may prosper through it. Poverty is a key of light to open the eye of the heart to the inexhaustible treasuries of God. One who has this key is the richest person in the world, for poverty is the door to richness. Those who pass through this door reach in their conscience the infinite treasuries of the Owner of All Property and discover that poverty is identical with richness. For this reason we can say, as Junayd al-Baghdadi did: *Richness is no more than the final, perfect degree of poverty.*[166]

When one is perfectly conscious of one's essential poverty before God and one's absolute dependence on Him, one is absolutely rich, for such a person no longer feels any need. This is what must be meant by the famous saying: *The real richness is the richness of the heart.* When one has attained this degree of richness, it is as if he or she has found a credit card that is valid everywhere. One who has such mysterious capital can be considered neither poor nor powerless. This is what is described in the following lines:

> His is power, by which we are powerful.
> We are well-known by His Name or fame.
> We go beyond peaks and continue our way;
> We overcome all difficulties with ease.

> We possess nothing worldly, but are absolutely rich,
> And are dignified and respectable with His Dignity.
> We follow the way of contemplation, so
> Whatever exists is a source of the knowledge of God for us.

---

[166] Al-Qushayri, *Al-Risala*, 273.

A Partial Glossary of Sufi Terms

Annihilation in God: A saint's seeing himself or herself as engulfed in the lights of God's Existence and as directed by God's Will; a saint's setting his or her heart wholly on God and never disobeying Him.

The Book: The Qur'an.

The Book of Creation or the Universe: The complete set of messages demonstrating God. The universe resembles a book: all of its "chapters" (systems), "pages" (skies, earth, other planets with their contents), "paragraphs" (seasons, days, months), "sentences" (genders, families, species), "words" (individual, existent beings), and "letters" (atoms or particles) point to God's Existence, Unity, Attributes, Names, and Acts.

Eternity: Being non-contained by time and space or by corporeality and material existence. It is also used to denote the eternal life in the Hereafter.

Free Will and Destiny or Predetermination: The first term denotes human free choice, and the other Divine Destiny. What is important to keep in mind concerning these terms is that God is not bound by such limiting human concepts as "time." For Him, there is no past, present, and future; everything is visible to Him at the same time. Therefore, what people perceive as "destiny," "fate," or any other word used to express the idea of predetermination is that one's human inclinations are brought into existence by God. In other words, one's free will is included in God's "determination" of events.

God's Attributes: God has three kinds of Attributes. The first kind consist of His Essential Attributes, which are Existence, Being Eternal with no beginning and end, Absolute Oneness (there is nothing like Him anywhere), and Self-Subsistence. The second kind consists of those Attributes that are inseparable from the Divine Being (Life, Knowledge, Hearing, Seeing, Will, Power, Speech, and the Power of Creation). The third kind consists of Attributes that, if they were to be found in Him, would be incompatible with His very Essence. Therefore, He is absolutely free of all such Attributes (defects).

God's Essence: The very Divine Being of God, God Himself, God as Divine Being.

God's Names: God has many Names that define Him. Each Name defines an "aspect" of the Divine Being, and is manifested in the universe to give existence to beings and events. Some of the Names are the All-Merciful, All-Compassionate, All-Creating, All-Seeing, All-Hearing, All-Powerful, All-Willing, All-Providing, All-Knowing, and the Giver of Life.

God's (Good) Pleasure: God's being pleased with one and approving of one's actions.

God's Supreme Throne: To make certain abstract truths understandable, the Qur'an introduces God as a king with armies and a throne. The throne, whose real identity and quality is unknown, may be considered the medium through which God directs affairs and governs the universe. For example, water is seen as the throne of life, for it is a means, even the origin, of life. Another example is earth (soil), seen as the throne of mercy, as God usually manifests His mercy through earth.

Initiate: A believer who is beginning his or her (spiritual) journey to God.

Master or Guide: The top teacher or educator in Sufism; one who educates and guides travelers or dervishes on their way to God.

Muhammadan Truth: The substantial truth lying behind all existence and especially Islamic principles; the truth represented by Prophet Muhammad, upon him be peace and blessings, as the Messenger of God.

" Faith journey "

Progressing or journeying, "from" God: A saint's being charged with conveying Divine commandments to others or guiding people to the way of God and on the way to God.

Progressing or journeying "in" God: A Sufi's continual travel in the manifestations of Divine Attributes and Names; his or her further travel to acquire full knowledge of God until annihilating his or her self in the Divine Will.

Qur'an: The Muslim Holy Book revealed by God, through the Archangel Gabriel, to Prophet Muhammad, upon him be peace and blessings, over a 23-year period.

Reaching God: A traveler's reaching recognition of God as the Creator, the Provider, the Merciful, the Just, and so on, and possessing a certain degree of knowledge of Him according to his or her capacity.

Soul or Self: In the Qur'an, both of these are called *nafs* - the carnal, lower self. Sufis gradually developed their own terms and hierarchy around this concept.

Subsistence with God: A saint's seeing himself or herself as subsisting totally by God's maintaining his or her life and governing his or her actions.

Sunna: The exemplary life of Prophet Muhammad, upon him be peace and blessings, and the set of norms he established for thinking, living, and worshipping in accordance with Islam.

Traveler: One who follows a Sufi system to reach God. Pilgrim / peregrine

Traveling "toward" God: A Sufi's following of a Sufi way or system of spiritual training until reaching God.

Union or Re-union: Finding and knowing God in one's heart or conscience. It also denotes acquiring full knowledge and love of God. It should never be mistaken or confused with such mistaken beliefs as incarnation and communion with or participation in the Divine Being. In Sufism, the world is the realm of separation, because one's spirit (his or her main existence) is not corporeal and therefore does not belong to the corporeal world. It belongs to the immaterial or metaphysical worlds, where Divine manifestations are clearer. In the other world, a person will know the realities, and be acquainted with Divine realities as they really are. That is why death is the first door to open onto this world and re-union with God after separation.

Unity of Being: An ecstatic saint's view of the creation as annihilated in God and of God as the true existent being. It should not be confused with monism and pantheism.

Way or Path: The Sufi systems of spiritual training.

World(s): There are countless worlds, each of which has its own particular features. For example, the World of Ideal Forms is the immaterial or semi-material dimension of existence where human deeds take on particular forms. The other world is the realm where people will go to either Paradise or Hell after being resurrected and judged. Immaterial worlds, in particular, have many different types. Again, each species, even each member of the human species, has its own world.

Bibliography

Abu Dawud, Sulayman ibn Ash'as al-Sijistani. *Sunan Abi Dawud.* 4 vols. Beirut, n.d.

Abu Nu'aym, Ahmad ibn 'Abd Allah. *Hilyat al-Awliya' wa Tabaqat al-Asfiya'.* 10 vols. Beirut, 1967.

Abu Talib al-Makki, Muhammad ibn 'Ali. *Qut al-Qulub.* 2 vols. Egypt, 1961.

Al-'Ajluni, Isma'il ibn Muhammad. *Kashf al-Khafa' wa Muzil al-Ilbas.* 2 vols. Beirut, 1351 AH / 1932 CE.

Al-Asqalani, Ibn Hajar. *Al-Isaba fi Tamyiz al-Sahaba.* 4 vols. Beirut, 1238 AH / 1910 CE.

Al-Bayhaqi, Abu Bakr Muhammad ibn Husayn. *Kitab al-Sunan al-Kabir.* 9 vols. Beirut, 1990.

Al-Bukhari, Muhammad ibn Isma'il. *Al-Jami' al-Sahih.* 4 vols. Beirut, n.d.

Bursawi, Isma'il Haqqi. *Tafsir Ruh al-Bayan.* 10 vols. N.p: Maktabat al-Islamiya, 1330 AH / 1911 CE.

Al-Darimi, 'Abd Allah ibn 'Abd al-Rahman. *Sunan.* 2 vols. Beirut: Dar al-Kitab al-'Arabi, 1987.

Dhahabi, Muhammad ibn Ahmad ibn 'Uthman. *Siyar A'lam al-Nubala',* 25 vols. Beirut, 1992.

Erzurumi, Ibrahim Haqqi. *Ma'rifetname.* Istanbul, 1300 [Ottoman Rumi calendar] / 1885 CE.

Al-Ghazali, Imam Abu Hamid Muhammad. *Ihya' al-'Ulum al-Din.* 4 vols. Egypt, 1967.

Gülen, M. Fethullah. *Kirik Mizrap.* Izmir: Nil Yayinlari, 1991.

Al-Hujviri, 'Ali ibn 'Uthman al-Jullabi. *Kashf al-Mahjub.* Tehran, 1979.

Harawi, 'Ali ibn Husayn. *Rashahat 'Ayn al-Hayat.* N.p., n.d.

Al-Haythami, Nur al-Din Abu al-Hasan 'Ali. *Majma' al-Zawa'id wa Manba' al-Fawa'id.* 9 vols. Beirut, 1967.

Ibn al-'Arabi, Muhy al-Din. *Al-Futuhat al-Makkiya.* 4 vols. Beirut, n.d.

Ibn al-Athir, 'Izz al-Din Abu al-Hasan 'Ali ibn Muhammad al-Jazari. *Usd al-Ghaba fi Ma'rifat al Sahaba.* 8 vols. Cairo, 1970.

Ibn al-Kathir, Abu al-Fida' Isma'il. *Mukhtasar Tafsir Ibn Kathir.* 3 vols. Beirut, 1981.

———. *Al-Bidaya wa al-Nihaya.* 14 vols. Beirut: Maktabat al-Ma'arif, 1966.

Ibn Hanbal, Ahmad. *Musnad.* 6 vols. Beirut, 1969.

Ibn Hibban, Abu Hatim. *Sunan.* 7 vols. Beirut, 1987.

Ibn Hisham, Muhammad. *Al-Sirat al-Nabawiya.* 9 vols. Beirut: Dar al-Ihya' al-Turath al-'Arabi, n.d.

Ibn Maja, Muhammad ibn Yazid al-Qazwini. *Sunan.* 2 vols. Egypt, 1952.

Ibn Sa'd, Muhammad. *Al-Tabaqat al-Kubra.* 8 vols. Beirut, 1980.

Al-Muhasibi, Abu 'Abd Allah Harith ibn Asad. *Al-Ri'aya li-Huquq Allah.* Cairo, 1970.

Mulla Jami', 'Abd al-Rahman ibn Ahmad. *Nafahat al-Uns.* Tehran, n.d.

Munawi, 'Abd al-Ra'uf. *Fayd al-Qadir.* 6 vols. Beirut, 1093 AH / 1682 CE.

Muslim, Abu al-Husayn Muslim ibn Hajjaj al-Qushayri. *Sahih al-Muslim.* 5 vols. Beirut, 1956.

al-Muttaqi al-Hindi, 'Ala al-Din 'Ali. *Kanz al-'Ummal fi Sunan al-Aqwal wa al-Af'al.* 8 vols. Beirut, 1985.

Al-Nasa'i, Abu 'Abd al-Rahman ibn Shu'ayb. *Sunan al-Nasa'i.* 8 vols. Beirut, 1930.

Nursi, Bediuzzaman Said. *Sözler.* Istanbul: Sozler Yayinevi, 1990.

Qadi 'Iyad, Abu al-Fadl. *Al-Shifa' al-Sharif.* 2 vols. Beirut: Dar al-Fikr, 1988.

Al-Qari, 'Ali. *Al-Asrar al-Marfu'a fi Akhbar al-Mawdu'a.* Beirut, 1986.

Al-Qushayri, Abu al-Qasim 'Abd al-Karim. *Al-Risalat al-Qushayriya fi 'Ulum al-Tasawwuf.* Cairo, 1972.

Al-Rabbani, Imam Ahmad Faruqi al-Sarhandi. *Al-Maktubat.* 1277 AH / 1861 CE.

Al-Rumi, Mawlana Jalal al-Din. *Al-Mathnawi al-Kabir.* 6 vols. Istanbul, n.d.

——. *Diwan al-Kabir.* 6 vols. 1957.

Al-Sharani, 'Abd al-Wahhab. *Al-Tabaqat al-Kubra.* Egypt, 1299 AH / 1881 CE.

Sivasi, Shamsaddin. *Manaqib Jiharyar Guzin.* N.p., n.d.

Al-Tabari, Abu Ja'far Muhammad ibn Jarir. *Jami' al-Bayan fi Tafsir al-Qur'an.* 30 vols. Beirut: Dar al-Ma'rifa, n.d.

Al-Tirmidhi, Hakim. *Khatm al-Awliya'.* Beirut, 1965.

Al-Tirmidhi, Abu 'Isa Muhammad ibn 'Isa. *Sunan.* 4 vols. Beirut, n.d.

Index